Raising Children to Love
Their Neighbors

Raising Children
to Love Their Neighbors

Practical Resources for Congregations

CAROLYN C. BROWN

ABINGDON PRESS / NASHVILLE

RAISING CHILDREN TO LOVE THEIR NEIGHBORS
Practical Resources for Congregations

Copyright © 2008 by Abingdon Press

This book is printed on acid-free paper.

Library of Congress Cataloging-in-Publication Data

Brown, Carolyn C. (Carolyn Carter), 1947–
  Raising children to love their neighbors : practical resources for
congregations / Carolyn C. Brown.
      p.   cm.
ISBN 978-0-687-65142-9 (binding: pbk., adhesive - lay-flat : alk. paper)
1. Child rearing—Religious aspects—Christianity.   2. Parenting—
Religious aspects—Christianity.   3. Love—Religious aspects—
Christianity.   I. Title

BV4529.B697   2008
268'.432—dc20   2007021812

All scripture quotations unless noted otherwise are taken from the New Revised Standard Version of the Bible, copyright 1989, by the Division of Christian Education of the National Council of the Churches of Christ in the United States of America. Used by permission. All rights reserved.

Scripture quotations marked GNT are from the Good News Translation in Today's English Version-Second Edition Copyright © 1992 by American Bible Society. Used by Permission.

What Does the Lord Require? words & music by Jim Strathdee, copyright © 1986 by Desert Flower Music, P.O. Box 1476, Carmichael, CA 95609. Used by permission.

Words for the song on page 92 from *Things to Make & Do for Advent & Christmas* by Martha Bettis Gee. Bridge Resources, 100 Witherspoon St., Louisville, KY 40202, p. 62. Used by permission.

llustrations on page 54-55, 60-61, and 67 by Robert S. Jones.

08 09 10 11 12 13 14 15 16 17—10 9 8 7 6 5 4 3 2 1

MANUFACTURED IN THE UNITED STATES OF AMERICA

Contents

Introduction

What Is This Book and How Can I Use It?

THE SEEDS OF THIS BOOK WERE SOWN during a conversation at a children's ministry committee meeting. The group was seriously involving children in the mission of their very mission-minded congregation. But someone observed that we tended to plan what we did with the children in response to whatever was going on in the larger congregation rather than consider what we needed to do to raise compassionate, mission-minded children. A schoolteacher jumped in, "What we need is a 'scope and sequence' for mission." We needed both a vision and a plan.

That was the beginning. Over the following years, the committee created a sequence of mission themes for elementary church school classes. The goal was that by the end of their elementary years, children would have experienced the care of others as a central activity of the church and would have personal experience with five basic ministries in which that care is extended. At the same time we were developing a series of mission projects that would be done once a month with preschoolers during the worship nursery hour. After moving from this congregation, I continued to work with and be worked on by the "mission scope and sequence project." This book is an attempt to share "where it is now" with the hope and expectation that it will lead others to take it further in their own congregations.

It begins with "A Vision for the Task." How do children grow in compassion? How can we lead them to love their neighbors? What should we be doing with children at which ages? The remainder of the book is made up of programs, activities, teacher workshops, even newsletter blurbs you can use in building your own scope and sequence for the children of your congregation.

"Resources for Raising Preschoolers to Love the Neighbors around Them" includes mini-workshops to help preschool teachers help their children build loving relationships with others in their class, a list of mission projects for preschoolers, and a collection of newsletter blurbs describing the work of preschool teachers, worship nursery volunteers, parents, even adult members of the congregation who are not parents, in terms of raising compassionate children.

"An Elementary Curriculum: Taking My Place among God's Loving People" is a detailed enrichment curriculum for Grades 1-5. A mission theme is assigned to each year. The expectation is that the class will add this to its regular curriculum of Bible study. Each theme includes information for teachers about how children understand that theme at that age, an introductory session, a list of hands-on projects from which to choose one or two, a list of "filler-type" activities for use in the class throughout the year, a celebratory summary session plan for the end of the year, and a resource list.

"A Word about the Partnership between Families and Congregations" explores the partnership between families and congregations as they raise children together. It includes a plan for a workshop for parents.

Start with the vision. Then pick from the "how to" ideas those that look as if they fit your congregation and its children. Build on them and adapt them. Some of the plans may work exactly as presented. Others will need to be adapted to fit your congregation. Still others will not work at all for you. It is also hoped that some will help crystallize your vision and suggest still new possibilities.

PART ONE

A Vision for the Task

"YOU SHALL LOVE THE LORD YOUR GOD WITH ALL your heart, and with all your soul, and with all your mind, and with all your strength. . . . You shall love your neighbor as yourself" (Mark 12:30-31). These are Jesus' two great commands. But at birth, human beings are creatures who experience ourselves as the very center of the known universe. Every person and thing around us is perceived to be either an extension of ourselves or a separate entity whose only focus in life is on us. How do we get from there to living like Jesus? And how do we help children do the same?

Jesus insists that we begin by seeing all people as neighbors. Luke makes Jesus' intention clear by following Jesus' proclamation of the two great commands with a question from the crowd, "But who is my neighbor?" to which Jesus replies with the story of the good Samaritan. Neighbors, his story claims, are people who take care of one other and everyone is our neighbor.

Loving neighbors is not easy in twenty-first century America. Individualism is prized. People of all ages are encouraged to develop themselves to their highest potential, to experience and grab as much of life as they can, and to look out for themselves. We, of necessity, warn even young children about "stranger dangers." The current national debates about torture, immigration, and who gets medical care pit self-protection against compassion with complex, convoluted arguments. In this environment, if we intend to love our neighbors and to teach our children to love their neighbors, we must be intentional. We need discipline. Actually, we need seven disciplines.

Seven Disciplines for Raising Children to Love Their Neighbors

Discipline is both a verb and a noun. The thesaurus lists as synonyms for the verb: instruct, educate, exercise, drill, prepare, train, regulate, teach, school.

It takes a little of all of those verbs to raise children to love their neighbors. We must instruct, teach, and educate them. We must exercise them, even drill them in order to prepare them for loving discipleship in this world. At times we must regulate their actions while we teach them to regulate their actions on their own. All the verbs make it clear that disciplining a child is a long-term commitment. You cannot instruct once and expect that the job is done. Instruction must be followed by exercises and drilling. What is understood clearly in one situation must be repeated and applied to new situations as they arise. Disciplining takes place over years until the discipline becomes part of life itself.

As children change and grow, our disciplining must also change and grow. Learning how to treat the other children in the preschool class becomes learning how to welcome the person of another race or economic background in elementary school. What is learned at one age becomes the foundation for new learning at the next.

Finally, as we undertake disciplining of our children, we often find that we must discipline ourselves. We must become more loving and neighborly. So, raising our children helps us grow as disciples. In many ways, disciplines are not tools for a task but a means of God's grace drawing us to love our neighbors more fully.

With that rich definition of discipline, I suggest the following seven disciplines for raising children to love their neighbors.

1. Teach relationship skills

The basic skills for loving neighbors at any age are the skills for building warm, trusting relationships. Pulitzer Prize-winning author Robert Coles, after interviewing young adults who were deeply involved in the American Civil Rights movement in the 1960s, concluded that the ability to form relationships with other people was more important for successful service than were high ideals. Being able to talk with and listen to another person and forge trusting relationships enabled workers to effectively stand beside the disenfranchised. Together they figured out what needed to happen next and did it. Workers without these neighborly relationship building skills tended to alienate the people they came to help by trying to incorporate them into schemes to achieve their own idealistic dreams. They were not very successful and often became quite frustrated and at times plain mean.

So, teaching children how to get along with other children is not teaching them to be "nice." It is equipping them with skills they will need to follow Jesus' number two rule. Figuring out how to take turns, share, play with other children, and hold a conversation with someone with whom you disagree is important work for young disciples. That work deserves our careful attention. Too often in children's church school classes we assume our central task is teaching Bible stories. Even in preschool classes we treat issues in relationships between children as problems that sidetrack us from our main task. But if loving our neighbor is one of our highest callings, then teaching children how to get along with their neighbors in the classroom may be our most important contribution to their education. Stopping everything to work through a relationship problem can be the most important lesson of the day. In that case, teacher training needs to include sessions on how to teach sharing and taking turns as well as how to present a puppet play or help children pray.

2. Model loving our neighbors

Not only do we help children relate lovingly with each other but we also model for them loving behavior. This is as simple (?) as disciplining our own behavior so that children can imitate what we say and do in relationships with our friends and with other people we encounter. Children do overhear and oversee everything we say and do. It is our job to make sure they hear and see the best.

Parents and other family members are the first models for children. Preschool teachers and caregivers follow. But as they grow, children also need to meet and know the congregation's experts at loving their neighbors. They can ride with the person delivering Meals on Wheels or watch the lady who arranges the sanctuary flowers into bouquets to take to sick members of the congregation. When it turns out that their favorite coach went on a mission trip or that their aunt is the lady who tutors children who cannot read, powerful connections are made. Children who meet and work with these caring heroes and heroines early and often expect that they, too, will be helping others all of their lives.

3. Practice loving neighbors together

Children not only overhear individuals but also they overhear their congregations. What congregations do together teaches children who they are and what they are to do. So it is important to include children in the life and ministry of the congregation. Though they do not understand fully what is going on, they learn by doing. The infant who first experiences the soup kitchen in an infant backpack and continues to work there with her parents as she grows never sees that place as "different" or "scary." The child who helps decorate the collection boxes, brings used clothes to put in the box, and watches the boxes fill up with the donations of others knows that sharing clothes is one thing Christians do. Scholar Joyce Mercer suggests that one task of congregations is to erect scaffolding on which children can climb around and through the congregation's activities. All that is required to erect such scaffolding is for planners of congregational ministries and activities to ask repeatedly, "How will the children be involved in this?" Planners for children's ministry help when they ask the same question and answer with plans that mesh activities that are especially for children with the life of the congregation. So, the stewardship campaign committee might ask, "How will we encourage children to support the church with money this year?" and a preschool class might make the table decorations for the congregation's stewardship dinner. As children participate in the loving ministries of their congregation, they grow in their understanding of what is going on and in their commitment to doing such work.

4. Tell stories of loving neighbors

Children learn by doing. They also learn through stories. Stories are safe places in which children can watch characters try out different activities and learn from their experiences. When we tell children stories about people succeeding and failing at friendships, we allow them to learn from the successes and failures of others. When we tell them stories about people loving their neighbors and then invite them to join the characters, we open them to new possibilities for taking care of others. When we tell them stories about the deeds of loving heroes and heroines, we inspire them to similar actions. There are innumerable stories. The Bible is full of them. Videos, DVDs, and books offer stories of great deeds of justice and compassion. Individuals can tell stories of what they have done. Teachers can tell stories of what the congregation is doing and invite the children to participate in the story in a specific way. All these stories encourage children to love their neighbors.

5. Introduce and use the vocabulary of compassion

Loving care has a vocabulary. At its heart are the words of relationships: friend, partner, forgive, kind, care, and so forth. But there are also vocabularies for special ministries of loving, including justice, hospitality, Meals on Wheels, donate, advocate, and others. When children know the vocabulary of compassion, they have the words to tell other children and adults what they are doing. The words also become the tools with which they analyze and interpret what they are doing. So, we must teach them the vocabulary of compassion.

6. Talk about using money to love our neighbor

In our culture talking about money is taboo. It is high on the list of topics not to be discussed at the dinner table. Preachers and congregants are relieved when the financial campaign with its discussions is completed for another year. We teach our children to be aware of what things cost, but not to tell others the price of our cool new sweater or shiny toy. But the fact remains that the way we use our money is one way we love or hurt our neighbors. Jesus talked about the use of money a great deal. We need to talk about it, too, maybe *especially* with our children. Children need to learn when and how to use money, and they need experiences in which they can share some of their money with others throughout their childhood.

7. Empower the children to love others and change the world

Loving a neighbor occasionally involves giving up something, but more often it involves learning to do something in a new way. I can grab the ball from you or we can play catch. I can eat interesting new foods when I make friends with an immigrant family. I am proud when I help collect money to buy a well that will save girls my age from carrying water in heavy jugs on their heads for miles every day. I can make a difference in the world by writing a letter protesting something unfair. When we teach children the skills to love their neighbors and invite them into the loving ministries of the congregation, we empower them. We prove to them that they are the powerful sons and daughters of God and the trusted disciples of Jesus Christ. They come to believe they can do important things that will make a difference.

These disciplines need to be part of childhood at all ages. They are, however, applied differently at different ages.

Disciplines for Raising Preschoolers to Love Their Neighbors

Jesus repeatedly insisted that we are all related. God created us to live together in healthy relationships with each other. When one flourishes, we all flourish. When one suffers, all suffer. Erik Erikson, who studied how children mature psychically, noted that the first task of childhood is to develop trust in the world around oneself. That trust is the result of loving relationships. If children are to love others, they must first experience the world and the people in it as loving and trustworthy.

Children spend their first days in their families, but many begin showing up at church very early. From the moment they appear in the nursery, the congregation has opportunities to convince them that the world is trustworthy and that they live in relationship to other people in the world. It is a slow process and calls us to apply all seven of the disciplines.

Teach relationship skills

Infants may perceive themselves as the center of the universe. But by the time they are school-age five years later, children need to be able to make friends, share, take turns, both forgive and accept forgiveness, and learn how to be part of a group. That is a huge order and requires a great deal of work. When it is well accomplished, children view the world as a trustworthy, friendly place and know that they can meet and interact with many people. When people say, "Everything I really need to know, I learned in kindergarten," they are referring to relationship skills.

Therefore, teaching those skills becomes the most important discipline the church can undertake with preschool children. Instead of training teachers to view the story time as their big teaching moment and free play for children as free time for adults, we need to train teachers to interact with the children on the playground and among the toys in order to help children learn skills as they negotiate the situations that inevitably arise. We tend to assume that any parent has figured how to do this. But, many have not. There are, however, experienced, well-trained preschool teachers who know insights, methods, and tricks that make a big difference. We need to share what they know with church school teachers and encourage them to use it to teach children relationship skills.

Introduce and use the vocabulary of compassion

One way we help children build relationship skills is to teach them the vocabulary of relationships. "Use your words!" we say repeatedly to encourage children to talk their way out of problems rather than push and pull their way out. We have to give them the words to use. They need words describing emotions and actions, "That hurt me!" or "You make me so angry!" These words help children describe the problems. They also need words that describe solutions and ideals, words like *friend, partner, share, take turns, kind,* and *gentle.* Preschoolers learn these words when they need them in the middle of the action. That means we must be there to say, "I saw you let Lee Lu have a turn with the truck. What a kind thing to do!" "I need two friends to . . ." See page 18 for a list of words to use frequently in classrooms. A mini-workshop suggests ways for preschool teachers to use them intentionally.

Practice loving neighbors

Loving our neighbor begins with learning how to get along with people around us. But it can quickly expand to include taking care of or helping others. When we ask children to take turns putting out cups and napkins and passing the wastebasket and talk appreciatively about what they are doing using the language of helping, we teach them to be helpers. Such simple helping is the foundation for service on a global scale later.

We can take this helping beyond the classroom by involving the children in simple ways in the congregation's helping ministries. When preschoolers bring canned goods to put in containers that are being filled by the whole congregation, they learn that church people bring food for others. Though they have almost no comprehension of the needs of the recipients, they are learning by doing what church people do. Furthermore, if as a class they take their cans to the collection center in the hallway, they build their familiarity with the building, recognize helping places in the church, and feel more at home and part of the church. Peter Benson of the Search Institute claims that for service to become a lasting disposition, it needs to be frequent—as often as weekly—throughout childhood and adolescence. That encourages us to make service, even with preschoolers, more than an occasional seasonal project.

Tell stories about loving neighbors

There are two ways to use stories to help preschoolers learn to love their neighbors. One is to tell stories in which children must sort out relationship problems. The story becomes the safe place where the children can work out how to deal with situations they face every day. Many preschool teachers present open-ended stories with puppets or flannel-board figures and invite the children to act out several potential endings and then to choose the best one.

Stories can also be used to introduce a service project. In a story, describe what you will do. Then, invite the children to do the project. Finally, retell the story, this time telling exactly what they just did. In the process, use your best compassion vocabulary to describe and interpret what you have done.

Talk about using money to love neighbors

Yes, even preschoolers are aware of money and are learning how it is used. They can be told that the church uses money to buy food and clothes for people who need them. Although they understand more fully bringing concrete objects like food for hungry people, they can also bring money to give to the church for buying food. Doing this gives them a chance to begin talking about money and to expect that such conversations will be part of church life.

Model loving neighbors

During preschool years, children learn most by watching and listening to what is going on around them. The discipline here is to discipline our tongues and actions to model the most loving behavior possible. This is not rocket science. All it requires is ongoing self-discipline exercised every day!

Empower children to love others and change the world

The other psychic tasks Erikson assigns to the preschool years are to find a balance between shame and autonomy and between guilt and initiative. Basically, preschoolers must find themselves to be lovable, capable individuals who can try new things knowing that sometimes they will succeed and other times they will fail and that is OK. They need to feel that they have what it takes to do what they need to do in their world. When we teach children relationship skills and involve them in important community-caring ministries, we teach them to see themselves as God's lovable and loving children. With this sense of identity and competency, they are ready for the expanding world they will encounter during their elementary years.

Disciplines for Raising Elementary Schoolers to Love Their Neighbors

Preschoolers are focused on their immediate world and the people in it. Elementary schoolers can see beyond their immediate world to the planet, even the universe. They are learning how this larger world works and finding their place in it. It is a critical time for the church to stand with them and show them how to love the neighbors they discover in their growing world.

Teach relationship skills

Friendships are very important during these years. But they are maintained largely by the skills learned in preschool. Occasionally it is necessary to stop everything and review basic skills for treating people lovingly. This work is important but largely a matter of applying the old skills in new situations with new people.

The fresh challenge is to help children find their places in a community whose understanding that all people are neighbors leads them to ministries of caring and justice. We must teach children that what applies to the treatment of people we know close at hand also applies to people at a distance. We must go with them to meet "different" people so that they can conquer their fear and learn how to love strangers like neighbors.

Practice loving neighbors

Elementary children want to do things rather than talk about them. This is especially true of the generation born since 2001, which already shows a pronounced preference for hands-on learning. Thus it is prime time for introducing children to specific caring ministries of the congregation by inviting them to participate in these ministries at greater depth. They are ready to explore the needs that call forth the collecting of goods and money. Their attention spans are longer and allow them to follow a project for months, enriching their understanding of it as they go. In the early grades, children participate in these ministries as members of the community. Doing so builds their sense of belonging to the church and their identity as a disciple who does what all disciples do. By the later years of elementary school, children are ready to learn leadership skills. They can create displays about projects, operate booths collecting items, even present a project to younger children or a minute for mission to the entire congregation. As they assume leadership roles, what was a communal commitment begins to become a personal one.

One newspaper published a series of articles about a dozen teenagers who had distinguished themselves in volunteer service in the community. The featured teens all told stories of formative serving experiences during their elementary years, often through their churches. Scientific studies agree that most adults who work actively on behalf of their neighbors as adults began that practice during the elementary school years. Congregations need to call elementary children in serving ministries.

Introduce and use vocabulary of compassion

Preschoolers need words with which to negotiate relationships with people around them. Elementary schoolers need words to explain and facilitate what they do. Each new ministry with which they get involved has a new vocabulary, e.g., homeless, shelter, soup kitchen, advocate, and beg. Giving them these words not only equips them to serve effectively, it also allows them to think meaningfully about the ministry and their role in it.

Tell stories about loving neighbors

Elementary-school children use stories much more richly than preschoolers. In biblical stories of loving neighbors, they can identify modern opportunities to act in the same way. They can use stories about people loving neighbors to analyze and understand what is possible in their own world and what they can do in similar situations. They gather heroes and heroines from stories of people who attempt to love others in significant ways. Reading and discussing a rich variety of stories gives elementary-school children deeper understanding of their world and how they can live in it.

Talk about using money to love neighbors

By the end of elementary school, children have a fairly full understanding of the use and value of money. Unless we talk about it openly and often, they will draw their conclusions from their own inexperienced judgments and from what they gather from the culture. So it is essential to include them in conversations about how we use money to love others as congregations and as individuals. First graders can understand bringing money to buy an animal for a family who needs it. Fourth and fifth graders can look at the church budget to identify for what the church spends its money. All these children are ready to talk about setting aside some of their money to care for others. Parents can help them set aside allowance money to keep a pledge to the church. Children can also set aside some of their "own money" from jobs and gifts to help others. Congregations need to speak to children as well as to adults about money and to respond to children's small gifts with the same receipts and appreciation with which they respond to adult gifts.

Model loving neighbors

As children's worlds enlarge, so does the field from which they draw their role models. Family members continue to be important. But children are also aware of other adults at work in their congregation. Opportunities to work with and be known by these people have great power. When an adult leader recognizes and encourages the work of a child, it has a big impact. And, of course, we all need to continue to discipline our tongues and deeds to model the most loving behavior for these critical observers.

Empower them to love others and change the world

Every time children do something new successfully and are appreciated for it, their willingness to try more grows. When congregations call them into caring ministries, listen to their ideas about that ministry, and let them know their involvement is appreciated, children grow in their ability and their commitment to loving their neighbors. Challenging them to take more and more leadership in caring for others is a congregational task. It is a wise plan to prepare a giving project before Vacation Bible School begins. It is even wiser to discard that plan in order to respond to a suggestion for giving that comes from the children during the week. Our job is to empower children to love their neighbors.

PART TWO

Resources for Raising Preschoolers to Love the Neighbors around Them

THE TWO PRIMARY DISCIPLINES FOR RAISING preschoolers to love their neighbors are teaching them relationship skills and inviting them to practice loving neighbors through simple service projects. The other disciplines tend to cluster around these two. This chapter provides three sets of resources for people working on these disciplines with preschoolers and their leaders:

- a collection of mini-workshops to help preschool teachers and nursery care-givers hone their skills for teaching children how to build loving relationships with children around them
- a collection of one-session serving projects for preschoolers
- a collection of blurbs describing preschool ministries in terms of raising children to love their neighbors

None of these collections is exhaustive. They are starter sets designed to suggest additions, adaptations, and further possibilities.

CHAPTER ONE

Mini-workshops for Teachers

THESE WORKSHOPS ARE CONSCIOUSNESS-RAISING sessions that redefine the teachers' task from classroom management, even drudgery, into teaching children the relationship skills that are the foundation of compassion. They accept the fact that children do not arrive in preschool classes able to relate easily to all around them and ready to hear Bible stories. So they call teachers to treat all the ins and outs of preschoolers at work and play together as opportunities to show them how to love neighbors in their class. The sessions are short—ten to fifteen minutes—unless a conversation really strikes a nerve or takes off in some other important way. They are good additions to the beginning of the quarter or unit teachers meetings. The workshops below are not in any particular order. They are simply a collection from which to pick ones that fit your situation at the moment.

Teach Preschoolers to Build Caring Relationships with Each Other

To encourage preschool teachers to be more intentional about how they work with children on developing relationship-building skills, present them with copies of "Young Children Learn How to Get Along with Others in Steps" (page 17). Walk more inexperienced teachers through the list, expanding on items as needed. Simply hand the list to experienced teachers.

Then challenge the teachers to make a list of guidelines for teachers who want to help children grow in their ability to relate to other people with love and compassion. For example, because three-year-olds "use words to describe everyday life and relationships," one guideline for them might be, "Engage in lots of conversations about what children are doing as they play. Use compassion words, like *kind*, *gentle*, and *loving* frequently." Teaching teams may work specifically on their own age group. Or the whole group of teachers may work through all the ages together.

In summary, note that some of our most important ministry to our children is not set out in the lesson plan, but is played out in how we interact with the children and help them interact with one other. When we pay attention to caring relationships, we are more in the business of raising compassionate Christians than of managing classroom behavior.

Introduce the Seven Disciplines for Raising Children to Love Their Neighbors

Read aloud Matthew 22:35-40 and Micah 6:8. Then ask teachers how we help children learn to live like this. Record their ideas in a column on newsprint or a blackboard.

Present the material about the seven disciplines beginning on page 4 as a short lecture, listing them on the board in a second column.

Invite the teachers to identify items on their list that match one or more of the disciplines. Add to your original list other ideas generated by the disciplines.

Close by rereading the two scripture texts and noting that part of our task as teachers is to help children learn how to live up to them.

Create a "Pitch In" Class

Teachers teach children to serve others by creating a classroom in which service is expected and praised. It is more efficient for adults to put snacks out for the children. But when one child puts a napkin at each place, another puts a cup at each place, another passes the trash basket at the end of the snack, the children learn the value of serving each other as well as enjoying a snack. After pointing this out, together make a list of classroom situations that are opportunities to teach children service, e.g., cleanup time, an unhappy child, a spill, getting supplies for a project to the table, and so forth. Ask teachers to identify specific ways to do this. Share methods, chart-keeping ideas, phrases to use in each situation, ways to respond to less than eager servers, and others.

Teach Preschoolers a Vocabulary for Caring Relationships

Give teachers a copy of "A Beginner's Vocabulary for Caring." Briefly walk through the words, explaining each one's ability to help a child relate to others with compassion.

Then ask individuals or teams to come up with phrases and sentences which include these words and which they could use in their classroom with the children:

"Shauna, that was a very kind thing to do."

"Look at the way you are taking turns! I am so proud of you."

Young Children Learn How to Get Along with Others in Steps

Two-Year-Olds . . .

Use words to name things.
May hit or grab when they cannot communicate with words.
Need help with words that show emotions—"You are angry because . . ."
Play well beside rather than with others.
Play pretend games using props and dolls.
Often prefer adult to peer relationships.
Have a growing sense of possession. "It is mine!"
Are totally me centered.

Three-Year-Olds . . .

Use words to describe everyday life and relationships.
Enjoy using words in chants and rhymes.
Are learning to listen but prefer to talk.
Still use muscles rather than thinking ability to solve problems,
       e.g., force the puzzle piece into place rather than turn it.
Enjoy other children but need time for parallel and solo play.
Are beginning to understand sharing and taking turns.
Are still me centered but are more able to conform to limits and adult demands.
Need adults sensitive to their feelings and ready to cover their embarrassment.
Need appreciation for their growing abilities and contributions to community life.

Four-Year-Olds . . .

Have a broad range of interests in people and their activities.
Have a growing recognition that other children are separate entities.
Show an expanding sense of self in bragging and showing off.
Regularly use language to communicate needs and solve problems.
Don't push, pull, or grab as much but do make wild verbal threats.
Enjoy working and playing with groups of two to three children.
Can be bossy and act very "grown up."
Share possessions and suggest taking turns—when it looks necessary.
Need adults sensitive to their feelings and ready to cover their embarrassment.

Five-Year-Olds . . .

Plan and play together in small groups.
Have some interest in playing simple games.
Want to have a "special friend" and feel left out when they do not.
Are developing respect for the rights of others.
Tend to be jealous of other children and compete for adult attention.
Engage in less physical fighting but more verbal aggression and name-calling.
Need adults sensitive to their feelings and ready to cover their embarrassment.
Enjoy small responsibilities and thrive on praise and affection.
Need firsthand experience to gain new information.

A Beginner's Vocabulary for Caring

kind, loving

gentle

share, sharing

taking turns

give

serve

I'm sorry—That's OK/ I accept/ I understand

help, helper, helpful

friend, partner, we, together

church—one place where we take care of others

"What a helper you are, Tim!"

"I need two friends to . . ."

Suggest that teachers post the words on a wall at adult eye level in their classroom and keep record of how many times they use them on a given Sunday. Finally, suggest that they listen for the children to use the words as an indication that they are adopting this vocabulary.

Teach Preschoolers to Share

Mini-lecture on how children learn to share:
Sharing is a key social skill for getting along in groups. It requires figuring out how to use resources and equipment with other people. Doing that is a lifelong discipline to which Christians are called. It is one way we "love one another." Contrary to what adults say to preschoolers, sharing is neither fun nor always easy. It takes creativity and commitment. Preschoolers are just learning the fundamentals and need our careful help.

The primary task of two- and three-year-olds is to learn to take care of themselves. During this time they are almost totally self-centered. For most two-year-olds sharing is all but impossible. Sharing can be imposed by adults but will generally be resented. Still, some children seem to share easily, almost naturally, during this time. For most children, however, learning to share is a hard, slow process that does not really begin until they are three. Because they think about themselves first, sharing is at first defined as what works for me, e.g., I'll play with the toy and you can watch or I'll play with the toy and you can play with it when I am done. By four, many children will share as needed. By age six or seven, most children understand sharing and cooperate with groups.

To encourage the process:

- When toddlers and two-year-olds want to play at giving objects to you and receiving them in return, play along and add appropriate words, e.g., "Thank you," "How kind of you to give that to me," "Would you like some too?" and so forth.
- Help children think about the needs and feelings of others, without reference to sharing, to build their awareness of other people, "Look at Gerry. What is he doing? How do you think he is feeling? I wonder why he feels that way."
- Identify as sharing activities that cannot be done alone, e.g., playing a game, marching in a circle to sing a song, working together to share a snack. (This makes sharing more than a matter of giving up solo use of toys and resources.)
- Catch children sharing and praise them in very specific, understandable words, "I saw you give the truck to Chris. That was a kind thing to do."
- Model sharing and describe what you are doing with words as you do it, "I brought some cookies from home. May I share one with you, Jamil? Would you like one, Janie? I like sharing cookies with my friends."

- Treat conflicts over toys among older preschoolers as opportunities to explore sharing ("How can we play with the truck together?") or taking turns ("Juan gets five minutes to play with the truck. Then Janet gets five minutes to play with it. I will tell you when it is your turn, Janet.")
- Invite the entire class of older preschoolers to work on a sharing problem that has arisen between two of them. Present the problem and ask for ways the two might play with the toy together, then give the two in conflict a chance to choose the best suggestion. Children learn the principles of sharing through the thoughtful handling of lots of specific situations.
- Plan activities with older preschoolers that require sharing, such as several children sharing a basket of crayons.
- Read books in which characters share.

Demonstrate a way of discussing sharing issues with children:
One way to help children explore sharing problems plaguing a class without putting anyone on the spot is to present the situation using puppets or flannel figures. Dramatically present the problem. Then ask the children to make suggestions. Act out a few of the suggestions and evaluate them as a group.

To introduce this process to these teachers, select one sharing problem to work through with them. Then challenge the teachers to do the same with another problem. Consider such problems as:

- Two three-year-olds want to play with the same toy.
- "She won't share!" screams a four-year-old as the girl next to her scoops all the crayons into a pile under her arms.
- Two children are fighting to get on the slide.
- Other situations the teachers offer.

Growing As Friends

Mini-lecture on friendship among preschoolers:
Jesus said, "Love your neighbor." He might have said, "Be a good friend." Friendship comes in many forms, but basic to all of them is appreciation of and loving concern for the other person. When we help children learn to be good friends to the other children in their class, we lay the foundations for lives of friendship, partnerships, and service to others. Doing this takes intentional work.

Children begin life experiencing themselves as the very center of the universe. Nothing exists except in relation to them, their needs, and their wants. As they realize that there are other separate beings and things out there, they must figure out what to do with and about them. Infants as young as six months crawl toward other infants on the floor to check them out. That is the beginning. Toddlers, even two-year-olds, generally play on their own, even in the middle of other children playing on their own. But, they soon express preference for pursuing this parallel play with certain children. As they learn to speak, *friend* is an early word and is applied to anyone in the room, especially when adults respond positively to their use of the word. Three- and four-year-olds have a fairly intense interest in friends and talk about friends a great deal. "Will you be my friend?" "My friend Joella played with me in the sand-box." "You are not my friend!" Even, "I hate you. You are not my friend." Though feelings do get hurt in all this talk, they heal quickly because the talk is more about how we play together than how we feel about each other.

To encourage the development of friendships:

- Point out and name the friendly things you see children do.
- Plan activities that require cooperation rather than competition, e.g., everyone adds their animal drawing to a mural of animals, play games passing a ball around a circle rather than relay races, and so on.
- Assign tasks for partners or friends to do together.
- Use lots of friendship words in class, like *friends, kind, together, we . . .*
- Read stories from the Bible about friends.
- Post pictures of young friends working and playing together at child eye level around the classroom.
- Help the children identify similarities and differences among themselves and learn to enjoy rather than fear the differences. This lays the foundations for tolerance.

When problems arise between young friends, talk about the problem. Treat these situations as opportunities to refine friendship skills.

1. Listen to each party tell their side of what happened and help the children listen to each other. The listening often clears up a misunderstanding at the base of the problem. It also provides time for emotions to subside.
2. After listening to both children, point out the problem and ask the children what they could do to solve it.
3. When a solution is agreed upon, send the children out to implement it.

Such discussions can be broadened to include other interested children or the whole class. In such discussions the plaintiffs are not "on the spot" but have a problem with which other children may be helpful. Other children must listen to the situation, and may then suggest solutions for the whole class to evaluate under the teacher's leadership. The children who presented the problem are then helped to choose from the possible solutions and to act on that choice. Even when there is a clear aggressor, the goal is to see why the aggressor acted as he or she did. When a misunderstanding is the cause of the altercation, more is gained by sorting out that misunderstanding and learning from it than by punishing the aggressor. When it becomes clear that the aggressor acted with malice or cold disregard for the other, the class may set a consequence that is more appropriate and has more impact than any teacher-imposed generic punishment. It takes a while for teachers and children to learn these steps, but with regular experience they take hold and work well in most situations.

Try out the suggested method for responding to friendship problems using one or both of these role plays. Give cards with assigned roles to two "children" and one "teacher." You may want to play each situation out several times trying class-suggested ways of dealing with the situation.

Situation One: "She pushed me!" "He grabbed at me!"

Four-year-old John: Susie has on a soft, fuzzy new sweater. You "touched" it to see how it felt. You are totally surprised when Susie gives you a hard shove. You start the play saying, "Teacher, Susie pushed me!"

Four-year-old Susie: You are wearing a new fuzzy sweater. While you are reading a book, John "grabbed at you." You did not like it at all. Upset, you pushed him away—hard!

Teacher: You did not see what happened but are confronted by two angry children, one claiming, "She pushed me!" and the other insisting, "He grabbed at me!"

Situation Two: "He knocked over our tower!"

Mike and Zeke: You two boys were happily building "the tallest tower in the world." When you stepped back to survey your work, George roared in and kicked it over.

George: Mike and Zeke have built a really tall block tower. As you look at it all you can think of is what a wonderfully loud crash it would make if it fell. So, when they step back from the tower, you roar in and kick it over. It does make a wonderfully loud crash. You are quite pleased until the two boys turn on you.

Teacher: One minute Mike and Zeke were building a tower. The next minute you saw George move in with a grin on his face and kick it over. You step into the action and start the role play by . . .

Conclude by pointing out that none of this is new. It just helps to remember that what we are doing is not babysitting or managing behavior problems or imposing discipline that we wish was better internalized by now in children. We are teaching children how to "love their neighbors." If they can learn it in preschool groups, they will have a better chance of being able to apply and develop their skills as they get older and move into the world.

Think It Through: "Good Behavior Is the Result of Good Relationships"

In her book *Postmodern Children's Ministry*, Ivy Beckwith says that among preschool children good behavior is the result of good relationships. Craig Dykstra in *Growing in the Life of Faith* says that what all people want to know is that we are loved and noticed. He further says that most sin is motivated by the desire to be noticed.

In other words, the children who cause the most trouble in classrooms are the children who have fewest strong relationships with other children and teachers in their class. They want to be loved and noticed. It suggests that if we want to improve their behavior, we need not punish them but instead help them build better relationships with others. To test this theory out:

1. Invite the teachers to write all of their children's names on a sheet of paper and draw lines between the children who have a good relationship.
2. Ask them to list the children who have the fewest connecting lines and assess whether these children have more behavior problems that those with lots of connecting lines.
3. Instruct teachers to make a list of friendship skills each of the identified children need in order to develop more lines of connection.
4. Brainstorm strategies for helping children develop those skills.

If there is another meeting of this group, agree to work on the strategies until that meeting and to compare notes at that time. Remember at the second meeting that learning social skills takes months, even years. Look for little signs of improvement rather than extreme makeovers.

Close with prayer naming each of the children in the class.

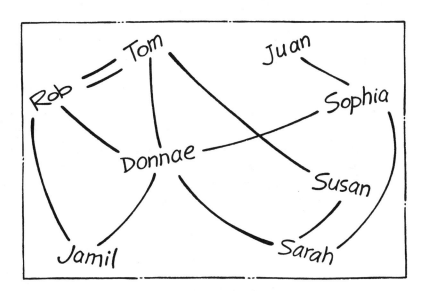

Communicating a Big Enough Job Description for Worship Nursery Volunteers

Most congregations work hard to get as many adults as possible involved in taking a turn in a worship nursery. Often this is seen as a thankless task, asking people to give up their time in the sanctuary to babysit children too young to behave properly in the sanctuary. It is presented as a baptismal DUTY, an unwelcome RESPONSIBILITY, even a NECESSARY EVIL. In asking for volunteers, the unspoken suggestion is that you are being called to an onerous but necessary task.

It doesn't need to be that way IF . . . we develop a vision of the job as an opportunity to talk with young children and to teach them compassion skills in a well-planned setting. We often do not have opportunities for training nursery volunteers, but we can communicate our larger vision of their work to them and to the whole congregation by the ways we invite them into this ministry and publicly thank them for their work. The paragraphs below are calls for worship nursery volunteers. They could be rewritten into paragraphs of appreciation to be printed where volunteers and others will see them or into blurbs for newsletters.

NEEDED: Adults and teens who know how to be friends to teach children those skills by being there, ready to step in when needed as children play on the playground or in their classrooms.

Teach tolerance and compassion and kindness and gentleness to preschoolers simply by being there on the playground or among the toys in the classroom to help them play together well. Children who learn how to share the blocks and negotiate conflicts in the dollhouse grow into diplomats and adults who serve their community. They cannot learn these things on their own. They need adult direction. You can shape the future of the world by spending a couple of Sundays this year with preschoolers at play during worship.

Children may learn to share when two of them want to use the same shovel at the same time or when it takes two to play on a seesaw. But they do not learn it on their own. They need experienced sharers to show them how it is done. You could be one of those sharing adults teaching the next generation to share. It is as simple as being there on the playground or among the toys in a nursery during worship on several Sundays during the coming year.

IT IS NOT BABY-SITTING!

IT IS TEACHING

TOLERANCE and COMPASSION and SHARING and KINDNESS

———————

Preschoolers learn by doing. They learn to share when two want the same toy at the same time. They learn how to be a good friend when they resolve conflicts with other children without coming to blows. They learn compassion when they respond to a child who is sad or hurt or needs their help. But they learn these important Christian ways of living only if there are adults around to show them how it is done. To be one of those adults, be a worship nursery volunteer!

———————

CHAPTER TWO

Serving Projects for Preschoolers

CHILDREN OVERSEE AND OVERHEAR WHAT IS going on around them. Our task is to introduce them to the life of the Christian community by letting them see and hear the church's missions of compassion that are going on all around them.

Service projects in preschool become like stories in which we introduce children to the world. Every project has a story, e.g., we read *A Rose for Abby* before making lunches for hungry people as she did or a Meals On Wheels driver tells about what he does before the children visit the pick-up spot on the back porch and make place mats for recipients. All the stories must be very simple and tell how we at church care for people.

These projects were originally designed to be used one Sunday a month during the worship nursery hour. Experience proved that children enjoyed repeating them year after year. A few favorites were used even more often. Because they were older each time they did a project, children understood it more fully. When they recognized projects they had done before, they were pleased to explain it to others. With each repetition their identity as a loving disciple grew.

Supplies for these projects include everything from the usual classroom art supplies to boxes of detergent and sandwich makings. The latter cost more than paper and crayons for craft projects. It is an expense that gets double value in that it both teaches the children and serves people in need. But it is too much to ask one person to pay repeatedly. So, plan ahead. Ask the Mission Committee to set aside a small amount for preschool mission projects in its budget or include a special line item in the Christian Education budget.

It also helps to gather and save digital pictures of people doing the work of the church and of members of the church staff at work. Choose pictures that include the tools the person uses and the setting in which they are used. Avoid group pictures of all the people who serve on a given project. Instead, choose pictures of one or two people actively involved in that project. These pictures can be printed large for children to see when they visit mission spots around the church and can be printed smaller at the center of a page that will become a thank-you card for someone who cares for others. Print pictures that will be reused on stiff paper and laminate them if possible. Collecting these photos is one good way for an adolescent or adult photographer to serve the children of the congregation.

Select—from the projects below and other projects they suggest—twelve that fit your congregation. Assign one to each month of the year, and you are ready to include preschoolers in your congregation's efforts to love your neighbors.

Put Stickers on Napkins for Fellowship Hour or a Church Supper

Offer children a chance to participate in the life of the larger congregation by putting stickers on napkins that will be used during the congregation's fellowship hour or a meal to be held that day after the service. Tell your adaptation of the story on page 29. Together, put the stickers on the napkins. (Choose seasonal or holiday stickers when appropriate or stickers of a church building or happy faces.) Then, as a class, deliver them to the spots in which they will be used. When the napkins are in place, pray together, thanking God for the church or for the holiday and asking God that the napkins will help people remember the holiday or love the church. To alert the congregation to the project and help them thank the children for their gift, print a notice in the worship bulletin, for example, "The napkins for today's fellowship hour have been decorated with stickers by the preschoolers as their contribution to our celebration of Easter."

Create Table Decorations for a Church Meal

Make table decorations for a church supper that follows worship that day. Begin by reading a book about the holiday the supper celebrates or about the church working together. Then, make the decorations. To create paper flowers to scatter across the table for a non-holiday meal, children glue precut construction paper petals onto precut round paper centers with glue sticks. Children may make as many as they wish. Some children will want to make one to take home. When all are ready, deliver the flowers to the dining area and place them on the tables. The flowers may be scattered in the center of the table or be set at each place as a coaster for a drinking glass. Before returning to your room, pray together, thanking God for the church.

Go on a "Treating the Saints Tour"

All Saints Sunday is a holiday celebrating all the saints of the church. It is a good time to introduce preschoolers to some of the saints of your congregation and the work they do. It is also the Sunday after Halloween trick or treating. So, define *saint* as someone who does God's work and then invite the children to go with you to deliver little packages of cookies, pretzels, or some other treat to the sites where saints do their work. It is trick or treat in reverse as children deliver treats. Before class, mount a photograph of each saint or group of saints at work on a big piece of colored paper titled "Thank you!" Invite the children to sign and decorate each card to leave with the treat. As the children move from place to place, ask them to look around themselves to guess what those saints do in this place. Fill in around

When the Church Meets for Fellowship Time

A Sample Story: Adapt It to Fit Fellowship Time at Your Church

When the church meets in the fellowship hall each Sunday . . .
  Mrs. Everett gets one cookie and a cup of coffee. She adds sugar to her coffee.
  Mr. Thomas with his cane goes to a chair. His friend brings him a cup of tea.
  Terrell doesn't get anything to drink, but he gets at least three cookies.
  Miss Pat doesn't eat anything because she is so busy talking.

Miss Pat isn't the only one talking. All over the room you can hear . . .
  "Hello. How are you today?"
  "What have you been doing this week?"
  "Did you hear what happened to . . ."
  "What do YOU think about . . ."
  "I am so glad to hear that you . . ."

Everyone talks to everyone else.
  People talk to old friends and meet new friends.
  Teenagers talk to other teenagers.
  Children laugh and talk together.
  Babies get passed from lap to lap.
  Old people talk with young people and children talk to old people.

All God's people are laughing and talking and eating together.
It is one special way we are church together.
What do you do when you go to fellowship hall?

After some discussion of what the children do and eat during fellowship hour, describe how the cookies and drinks are prepared each week and who prepares them. Then suggest that we can help make it special by adding stickers to the napkins today.

their guesses with information and photographs of those saints at their work. Together, set out the treat bag and the thank-you card. Then say a brief prayer for that group, or person, before moving on. Younger children visit only one site. Older classes may visit three or four. Include some of the saints on staff and some volunteer saints. Possible saint spots to visit include, but are not limited to:

- minister's office—see the telephone for talking with people, the computer for writing sermons, and all the books to help think of good things to say
- receptionist—see the fancy phone for transferring calls to the right person
- choir room—see the piano and choir robes
- Meals on Wheels pick-up point—see coolers, food containers
- clothing or food collection points
- table where volunteers prepare the church newsletter for mailing
- kitchen where meals are prepared
- cabinet where supplies are kept for preparing flowers to be taken to sick members of the church after Sunday worship

Back in your room, share a snack of the same treats you left on your tour because the children are also saints of the church. (Beyond introducing children to the work of the congregation, this activity builds their familiarity with and sense of comfort in the church building. This is especially important in larger congregations in which young children tend to stay in one area of the building.)

Lay Ministry Sunday Scavenger Hunt

This is a variation on the Treating the Saints Tour, above. It is best done with four- and five-year-olds who have been on the previous tour. Begin this tour in your classroom with the fingerplay, "Here Is the Church," and noting that the most important part of a church is people. Then work with a set of clues that direct you to the first stop on your scavenger hunt. Give each clue one at a time, encouraging the children to guess who the person is and where his or her spot is. Once they figure it out, go to that place. There you will find clues for the next place. At the final stop leave clues about the children's class that will send them back to their classroom. Use clues such as these for the flower distributors:

- We think flowers are beautiful!
- We want to let people who are sick know we love them.
- We deliver. What we deliver makes people happy.
- The name of a parent of one of the children who works in this ministry.

Here Is the Church Fingerplay

Here is the church	*Fold hands together with fingers inside*
Here is the steeple	*Form steeple with first finger of each hand*
Open the doors	*Open both thumbs outward*
Here are the people.	*Open hands and wiggle fingers*
You can have a church	*Fold hands together with fingers outside*
And not have a steeple	*Keep fingers in place*
But you can't have a church	*Shake your head*
Without any people.	*Open thumbs outward to show empty palms*

Make Cards for and Decorate the Door of Those Who Clean the Church

To raise awareness of and appreciation for the work of the people who keep the church clean, talk with the children about what is involved in doing that job. Then show them photographs of the people who keep your building clean. Be sure the children know their names and tell both about their work and a little about them as people. Then make cards thanking them for their work. Help the children tape their cards around a big sign on which you have printed, "Thank you, [NAME/S], for keeping the church clean" on these cleaners' office or the main cleaning supply closet. If the logistics work in your situation, kindergartners may do one cleaning task such as emptying all the preschool garbage cans for that one day as a way of both helping and thanking the cleaners.

Recycle this project to thank and build awareness of other "less recognized" church workers, such as receptionist, kitchen crew, yard mower, and so on. These workers may be volunteers or paid staff.

Communicate with Other Children Who Use Your Room

Many young children's church school classes share their space with one or more weekday groups of children. Sharing our space is one way we share. Build a relationship between the two groups who share your space to help the children see benefits as well as requirements in the arrangement.

At the beginning of the year, spend some time looking around the room with the children to see what you can learn about the other children who meet here during the week. Read names on the cubbies or mailboxes. Look at some of their art and displays on the walls to learn what they do when they are here. Then make a big Sharing Friends Poster to introduce yourselves to the other group. Mount some photos of your class doing some of the things you do together and add captions dictated by the children. Invite older children to write their names on the poster. In the center write a greeting message, for example, "Hello, we are your Sunday friends. We are happy to share this room with you." Gather around the completed poster for a prayer. In the prayer, name each of the children in your group and each of the children in the other group, asking God to watch over all of you. Then, leave your poster in a prominent place for the other class to find. If possible, suggest to the other group's leaders that they make a similar poster in response.

Near Valentine's Day repeat the process of looking around the room to see what your friends who use the room during the year are doing now. Then make one poster-sized valentine for them. Draw a big red heart in the middle of a sheet of white poster paper. Add photos of yourselves, valentine stickers, and heart stamps using sponge hearts or cookie cutters. Write messages to children "Hi, [NAME]!" or "We like to play with the [NAME OF TOY] in the room too"!). Put the poster in an obvious place in your room for the other group to find.

Play a Valentine game. Hide red paper hearts around the room. Then invite the children to look for them. This can be played several times. Finally, hide the hearts for the other group and leave a message telling the other group how many hearts are hidden in the room and urging them to find them.

On any Sunday, talk during clean-up time about leaving things ready for the other group and point out ways they left the room clean for your group.

Make Cards to Be Delivered to the Sick and Homebound

Preschoolers can make the covers for cards that will be delivered to sick or homebound members of the congregation with flowers from Sunday or at holiday times. Adults charged with this ministry write notes on the cards possibly referring to the children's art on the cover.

At Thanksgiving, begin seated around a large piece of paper. Draw around each child's hand inviting them to write their name on their hand and color it as they wish. As you work, talk about what you all do together at church. Add other hands for church leaders they know, such as their choir director or the pastor. As the project winds down, point out that some people must remain at home and cannot come to church to be with their church friends. Invite the children to make cards that will be sent to these people so that they know their church friends love them. To make the card covers, help each child draw around his or her hand on a prefolded card cover and glue a feather to each finger creating a thanksgiving turkey's tail. On the thumb add a google eye to make the turkey's head. Children may want to add additional features with markers. If they want to add their name, have them do so on the cover, saving the inside of the card for the adult note.

At Valentine's Day begin a card cover project by reading *Somebody Loves You, Mr. Hatch.* Talk with the children about valentines they will share and invite them to make valentines for people who, like Mr. Hatch, live alone and will not likely get any valentines. Then decorate the front of prefolded cards with red hearts. Younger children can press heart-shaped cookie cutters or sponges onto stamp pads made by pouring liquid tempera paint onto folded paper towels laid in a Styrofoam meat tray. Older children enjoy tracing heart stencils with red markers or combining a variety of heart stickers into pleasing patterns. The older children may deliver their cards to the spot where flowers are divided for delivery. Younger children (or makers of cards too gooey to transport) can leave their cards in the classroom for someone to move once they are dry.

At Easter begin with the word "Alleluia!" Say the word together and sing any songs the children know that include the word. Point out that it is a word we say over and over on Easter day. Then, note that some people will not be able to come to church on Easter. To be sure that they get an "Alleluia!" make Alleluia Easter cards for them. Preprint the card covers with the word "Alleluia!" Invite the children to add a variety of Easter and flower stickers around it.

When the cards are ready, deliver them as a class to a central basket. Tell the children about the people who add messages to and mail the cards. If possible, have photographs of people doing this work or have a person seated with the basket to receive the cards, thank the children, and tell them how the cards will be used.

Feed the Birds

Birds, as well as people, are our neighbors. Read a children's picture-book version of the creation story. After reading the whole book, go back to the page on which birds are created. Point to the birds and begin a conversation about where the children see and hear birds and what birds need to survive. Then make pinecone bird feeders to hang on a tree in the churchyard. Before class, tie string hangers onto pinecones and mix equal parts of vegetable shortening, lard, or suet with oatmeal or cornmeal. (One half cup of each makes enough for one large cone or three smaller ones.) During class the children spread this mixture on the pinecones with plastic knives, then roll them in birdseed spread out on a tray. (This is a messy project, so have clean-up supplies handy.) Place finished feeders on a tray. As a class, take the tray outside, hang the feeders, and pray for the birds that will eat from them. (This is a project for colder weather when birds really need the feeders and the fatty mixture will not melt off the cones.)

Collect Baby Supplies for a Shelter—
Especially at Christmas but Also Other Times

During December, build on the stories about the baby Jesus by collecting baby-care supplies (wipes, bottles, formula, clothes, toys, and so on) for a local shelter for homeless families or women. Encourage parents to help the children shop for their contribution and bring it to their class. A person from the shelter may be willing to come receive the supplies from the children and show them pictures of the babies who will use the supplies. Or the person who delivers the supplies could take pictures of themselves making the delivery to show to the children the following Sunday.

A Possibility: If the fourth-grade class is working with the homelessness theme in the elementary-school curriculum in part three of this book, they have directions for leading a baby-care products collection with preschoolers. It is designed to help them learn how to plan and carry out such a drive and to give them a chance to be attractive models to younger children. So check in with the fourth graders about leading this project.

A Warning: Be sure that the shelter you plan to contribute to has storage to receive bulky items like disposable diapers. It is quite possible for a middle-size congregation to collect more diapers than a shelter can store. In such a case, you'll need to ask for smaller items.

Decorate and Fill Snack Bags for a Soup Kitchen

Soup kitchens or shelters for the homeless are generally happy to have a box of zippable plastic bags filled with snacks. Homeless patrons can slip one in a pocket for later in the day. Hungry people, especially hungry children, can munch on one while they wait for a meal or appointment. Making such bags is fun for preschoolers.

Begin by reading the story "Allen and Suzanna Move" on page 35. Adapt it so that the family moves to your town and finds themselves at the center to which your snack bags will be taken. If possible show the children photographs of that center. Then wash hands. When hands are clean, add seasonal or welcoming stickers to snack-size zippable plastic bags. Help the children take turns pouring several kinds of cereal and small pretzels into a large mixing bowl and scoop the mix into the bags. Pack the bags in a box. If several classes are participating, pack all the bags in one big box in a central place. When the box is full, gather around it to pray for the people who will eat the snacks. Then enjoy your own snack of the same mix.

Make and Pack Sandwiches—Even Sack Lunches

Read *Uncle Willie and the Soup Kitchen, A Rose for Abby,* the "Tony and Terry Feed Hungry People" story printed on page 36 for the youngest children, or the story of Jesus feeding the multitudes. Then tell the children about the project. When the project is complete, gather around the packed food for a short prayer for the hungry people who will eat it. For a snack, enjoy quarter sandwiches just like the ones you made.

Make sandwiches that can be delivered for immediate use or frozen for future use by a soup kitchen. On a long table set out open loaves of bread, open packages of sandwich meat (with slices separated and fanned out for easy pick up), open slices of cheese (also fanned out), and zippable plastic sandwich bags, in that order. (Do not spread with mustard or mayonnaise. The center may provide them or you can drop packets of each in the bags.) After washing their hands children form a line and move down the table, each picking up two slices of bread, adding the meat and cheese, and putting the sandwich in a bag. An adult checks the bag closure. The child puts the sandwich in a box and returns to the rear of the line to repeat the process.

To make sack lunches, the three-year-olds wash and dry apples, putting one in the bottom of each sack, the four-year-olds mix and fill small bags of snack mix, and the five-year-olds make the sandwiches. The sacks are filled in the church school hallway and then packed in boxes to go to the center.

Most soup kitchens and shelters need a steady supply of such sandwiches. Contact your local centers to learn what kind of sandwiches or sack lunches they need and how they should be packed.

This project can be done on any Sunday, but it is especially effective on a Sunday when older children and adults are participating in a hunger walk. On those days it gives younger children a chance to be part of the whole congregation's ministry of feeding the hungry.

Allen and Suzanna Move

Allen and Suzanna lived in the mountains of Tennessee with their mom and dad. There was a creek by their house and lots of animals in the woods around their house. But there were no jobs.

One day Dad came home with a smile on his face. "We are moving to Atlanta," he said. "I have a job there. We need to be in Atlanta next week."

The next two days they worked hard. They packed their clothes. Allen and Susanna each had to pick five toys to take with them. Mom packed sheets and plates and all their pictures. They packed everything they could into their car. Then they climbed into the car. Dad bowed his head and they all prayed, "God take care of us as we move to Atlanta. Amen." Then they drove away. They rode and rode and rode. Everyone was tired. When they got to Atlanta, there were cars and people everywhere! They got very lost. Finally, Dad pulled into a parking lot to think. Then he went into Cafe 451 to ask some questions.

When he came out his smile was back and he had four bags of snacks in his hands. "We just thought we were lost," he said. "God brought us straight to the right place. Cafe 451 is church people. They are going to give us lunch, then help us find a place to stay."

Allen and Susanna ate their snacks while they waited for lunch. At their table, Dad prayed, "Thank you for a new home in Atlanta and for food to eat. Amen."

Tony and Terry Feed Hungry People

Tony and Terry went to church every Sunday. There was always something important to do in their room. Most days they sang songs and heard stories. Some days they made pictures or played games. One day they made sandwiches for hungry people to eat.

First, they washed their hands.

Then they put one piece of meat and one piece of cheese between two pieces of bread.

Each sandwich went into its own bag.

They made lots of sandwiches.

When they finished, they put the sandwiches in a big box. The box was taken to a kitchen where hungry people came to get food. The people who came the next day were so happy to find the big box of sandwiches! Each person stuck a sandwich in a pocket.

No one would be hungry today!

Everyone was happy.

Decorate Cookies for Shut-ins, Church Staff, a Soup Kitchen, and Others

Ice and decorate simple sugar cookies for hungry people. Pack them in shallow boxes to send to a local shelter, senior center, soup kitchen, or other local mission effort that could use some cookies. Or arrange them on paper plates, add a simple thank-you note, and deliver as a treat to church workers. Younger children enjoy spreading icing with plastic knives on round cookies then adding a few sprinkles. Older preschoolers also enjoy drawing flowers, stars, and seasonal figures on cookies by squeezing icing from tubes. After icing, packing, and delivering cookies, eat some as a snack.

Pack Detergent in Individual Bags for Homeless People

Put preschoolers' love of scooping to work for homeless people who need small packages of detergent. Begin with the children by opening your Bible to Acts 9:36. Point to the name Tabitha. Then tell the following story about her.

Tabitha's Gift

Tabitha was a member of the church at Joppa. She spent all her time taking care of people. She worked hard to be sure everyone had nice clothes to wear.

If you told someone at church that they were wearing a handsome shirt, that person would probably smile and say, "Yes, it is handsome, isn't it? Tabitha made it for me. It is very special to me."

Another person would say, "See my pants? They had a big hole right there. Tabitha patched the hole and made a pocket over it to hide the patch."

A mother with five children would say, "What would we do without Tabitha? She can take an older child's ruined dress and turn it into a fine shirt for her little brother! I don't know how she does it."

Making and fixing clothes was Tabitha's gift. She did it well and she liked doing it. Tabitha used her gift to take care of people who needed good clothes.

After telling the story, invite the children to help people get their clothes clean. Point out that people who do not have a place to live have a very hard time keeping their clothes clean. Pass a big box of detergent among the children. Ask how hard it would be to carry it with you everywhere you went every day. Then pass around a small zippable plastic bag of detergent and ask whether they would rather carry the box or the bag. Invite them to help turn the big box of soap into lots of little bags that will be given to people at a soup kitchen or shelter. If possible, show them pictures of people at that center. Pour the detergent into a large mixing bowl from which the children scoop soap into small zippable plastic bags. If you wish, let the children decorate the bags with stickers before filling them. Gather completed bags in a box and pray for the people who will use them to get their clothes clean.

Warning: Avoid detergents with strong perfumes. They can be overwhelming to sensitive noses working in small rooms.

Make Meals on Wheels Place Mats and/or Tray Favors

Begin by opening your Bible to John 6:1-12 and telling the story of Jesus feeding the crowd in your own words or by reading the story from a storybook. Then introduce Meals on Wheels as one way your congregation feeds people too.

If you have a pick-up location at your church, take the children to see the coolers there. If possible, fill one of the meal containers with plastic food from the children's play kitchen and display photographs of a member of your church making a delivery nearby.

If your class is small and you do not have a pick-up location at your church, take the children to sit in your car. Tell them about people who get in their cars and take food to hungry people every day.

If possible ask a church member who delivers Meals on Wheels to meet the children (either in the classroom, at the pick-up spot, or in their car) to tell them about this ministry.

Sample Story

(adapt to fit a Meals on Wheels team in your congregation)

Every Tuesday Mr. and Mrs. Jones come to the church in their van. They pick up one big cooler filled with lunch bags and juice boxes and another big hot box filled with boxes of hot food. They also pick up their list of names and a map of where each person on the list lives. There are twelve people on the list. The Joneses really do not need the list because they generally deliver food to the same people every week and know everyone. Once they have everything in their car, they start driving. At the first stop they see Mrs. Smith. Mrs. Smith is ninety-years-old and is very tiny. She lives alone in a small house. When the Joneses bring her lunch, she is happy to see them and has something funny to tell them. At the second stop the Joneses leave dinner for Mr. Jim. Mr. Jim cannot get out of bed without help. A nurse comes each day to help him. She will see that he gets his good, hot lunch from Meals on Wheels. Everyone they take food to is glad to see the Joneses, and the Joneses are glad to see them. They have become friends. Today we can send a gift along with the food the Joneses are taking. We can make . . .

Make place mats for the recipients of the meals. Before class print the God is Great Prayer in the middle of several sheets of paper and cut out lots of food pictures from magazines. During class invite children to glue the pictures around the words on the place mat. Use glue sticks rather than liquid glue for quick drying. Teachers then sandwich each place mat between two sheets of clear contact. Trimming the edges with pinking shears is a nice finishing touch, but trimming with plain scissors also does the job.

At holiday times, repeat the storytelling and make small crafts to send along as tray favors. Repetition builds familiarity with Meals on Wheels.

CHAPTER THREE

Blurbs for Teachers and Parents (with the Whole Congregation Listening In)

ONE WAY TO SENSITIZE TEACHERS, PARENTS, AND other adults in the congregation to what is involved in raising children to love their neighbors, is to print short blurbs in newsletters, on the website, among the announcements in the worship bulletins, wherever people might notice. In each blurb describe one well-recognized preschool issue or dilemma, interpret it in light of raising compassionate Christians, and suggest appropriate responses. The goal is to help people see the congregation's work with preschoolers not as dealing with wiggly, dirty, unpredictable little people so that the big people can be "church" together, but as intentionally directing children to grow as compassionate Christians. Blurbs call preschool teachers to see their ministries in the loftiest of terms, remind parents of the importance of the nitty-gritty "keeping after it" they do with their children, and call non-parents to be supportive of both the children and their adults. Some blurbs can even go in youth newsletters to alert teenagers to their responsibility to their younger brothers and sisters in Christ. Below are sample blurbs.

Children have to learn how to be gentle. They need to be shown and told how to touch the baby or play with the puppy or play with another child. Actually, they need to be shown and told many times. That is how they learn to be gentle and one way they grow as compassionate Christians. Teaching gentleness is a baptismal responsibility for church school teachers, nursery volunteers, parents, and all the rest of us when we are around young children.

_____

Children who learn to speak respectfully to all people—even when they are angry—grow into adults who speak respectfully to all people—even those on the other side of the argument, even when they are angry. Teaching children to speak respectfully to all other children, to their teachers, and even to their parents is important to the future of the world!

_____

———————

Toddlers don't have long-term memory, so parents and teachers have to model Christian practices, say what is right, and redirect activities again and again and again. That is how young Christians grow. It is also how parents and teachers learn patience. "Thanks!" to everyone who raises young Christians in our preschool classes and nurseries. "Hang in there!" to parents who raise them day and night at home.

———————

Forgiveness is near the heart of the Christian faith and life, but it doesn't come easy. Parents and teachers walk children through the apologizing and forgiving cycle every day, some days many times. They do this to teach children to recognize their mistakes, to say I'm sorry, to forgive others when they say they are sorry, and even to accept forgiveness from others. Sometimes it is easier to do than others. Often, it takes the wisdom of Solomon to decide when to push a child to say "I'm sorry" or "That is OK" and when to wait until she is truly sorry or it is really OK with him. It also takes both courage and humility to teach a child forgiveness by apologizing to him or her when you are in the wrong. When we do all this work, we are the hands and feet of Jesus for our children.

———————

Teach children the vocabulary of compassion by using it every day in conversations with them. *Kind, help, give, share, care, love, partner, friend, helper* are words that shape preschoolers' understanding of the world and their place in it when they use them every day. Kindergartners are ready to add the big word "responsible." All of us can teach children the vocabulary of compassion by using those words in their presence.

———————

At least at church: When children want to shoot guns or turn whatever is available into a weapon, the rule is you can shoot at a target (block on a shelf, a block tower, etc.) but not at a person, not even a "bad guy" or animal.

———————

Getting children to help in class by putting out cups, napkins, and cookies for snack and by picking up toys at the end of the morning is not so much teaching manners as it is teaching Christian service. (the short version)

———————

Getting children to help in the room putting out cups, napkins, and crackers for snack and picking up toys after we use them is teaching Christian service. So intentionally assign chores and oversee the care given classroom toys. It is a good way for children to begin contributing and being counted on in the classroom and at home. When they ask "Why?" the answer is "Because we are a class and we work and play together" or "Because we take care of the things we use here." (the more complete version)

———————

To raise compassionate children, catch them in the act of being compassionate. Name and point out kind, caring actions when you see them. Tell them what they have done and praise them for it. Give them words to describe their loving, caring, sharing deeds. All this positive reinforcement is a powerful encouragement. You don't even have to be a parent or teacher to do this. Anyone can catch children being compassionate anywhere around the church and let them know. It is one way we keep our baptismal promises to them.

Name-calling: Children may get away with calling someone "poopoo head" on the playground or even at home. But at church we teach them that God made and loves every person. So, there is no name-calling of any kind, ever, not even as a joke. Teachers intervene on the first offense, reminding children of the rule and its reason. "You don't have to like her, but you do have to speak kindly to her."

When imposing consequences on a preschooler for bad choices and actions, state the reason for the consequence in simple theological terms.

"You may not hit Kenny. God loves him just as God loves you."

"In this room we do not take things from other people. We share."

"You don't have to like her, but you must treat her kindly; you may not pull her hair."

Though they will change their ways mainly to avoid the unwanted consequences, the children also begin hearing why compassionate people act as we do.

(Perhaps after a well publicized disaster . . .) When confronted with a painful tragedy on TV or face to face, soften the sting and set the stage for compassion by directing a preschooler's attention to the heroes—the firefighters, police officers, medical personnel, and so on. Shortly after 9/11 a mom reported that her twin four-year-old sons rushed canned sodas out to the garbage collectors saying, "Thank you for everything!" They had a bit to learn about which heroes do what, but they were well on their way to compassionate response. And what garbage collector wouldn't appreciate such a gift!

It's stewardship season. Preschool children grow into Christian stewards by picking up their toys, helping clean up after snacks, and learning how to treat animals around them. It's a slow, repetitive process for parents and teachers every day. Preschoolers also begin learning about using money to take care of people by bringing coins to contribute to projects at church. Parents can hand a child a coin, saying something like, "Take this to church. The church will use it to buy food for hungry people." Teachers as they help a child put the coin in the offering say, "Thank you. The church will use that coin to take care of God's people."

———————

During December our culture encourages children (and the rest of us!) toward greediness and self-absorption. "What will I get for Christmas?" becomes the key question of the month. To help counter that, teachers and older friends can discipline themselves to not ask children the automatic question "What do you want for Christmas?" Instead ask, "What will you do for Christmas?" or "Do you have any special gifts to give someone for Christmas?" Also, plan times when children can focus on giving rather than getting. This year at (CHURCH NAME), we invite you to . . . (LIST PLANNED PROJECTS).

———————

This is obviously a starter list. Add to it based on what you want to raise with the teachers, parents, and other members of your congregation. These blurbs are concerned with raising compassionate children, but other blurbs might describe how children grow as worshipers or fellowship hour participants or . . . the list is almost endless.

PART THREE

An Elementary Curriculum: Taking My Place among God's Loving People

THE PRESCHOOL YEARS ARE ABOUT LEARNING to love those around us and being introduced to the church as a community that loves people beyond itself. The elementary school years are devoted to learning about the larger world and to learning how to take our places in it. That makes the elementary years prime time for learning by participating in the missions of the church. Part one, "A Vision for the Task" explains why this is so. The following curriculum is one congregation's "how." It began as an enrichment curriculum to be used with the denomination's curriculum for grades one through five Sunday school. Each grade is assigned one mission theme.

First Grade	We're Responsible for the Animals
Second Grade	Sharing So Every Body Has Enough (Food, Water, Medicine . . .)
Third Grade	It Is a Global Neighborhood
Fourth Grade	Helping the Homeless
Fifth Grade	It Is Not Fair! Standing Up for Justice

The goals of the curriculum are that by the time they enter adolescence, children will:

- know about and have experience in a variety of the church's efforts to love other people
- have a basic vocabulary for participating in the mission life of the congregation
- understand themselves as persons who have the power to make a positive difference in the world around them
- have a sense of connectedness to and concern for other people
- have basic skills for participating in the congregation's mission work

The curriculum was originally designed to be used in the classroom model. All classes did the introductory and summary sessions on the same Sundays, then pursued projects and filler activities on their own schedules. In congregations using the rotation model, the sessions could be led by the shepherds during scheduled breaks between units. A single theme could be pursued during weekday gatherings of children or could be added as enrichment to a Vacation Bible School curriculum.

In broadly graded groups, plan the use of themes thoughtfully. The fifth-grade justice theme is beyond the understanding and experience of most first graders. The animal theme would insult most fifth graders. So when working with younger elementary groups use the first-, second-, or third-grade themes. When working with older elementary groups use third-, fourth-, or fifth-grade themes. When working with kindergarten through fifth graders in one group, use the second-, third-, or fourth-grade themes.

The Format

For each grade there is an introductory session plan, a list of potential projects, a list of filler activities for use during the year, a summary session plan, and a resource list.

The Introductory Session identifies and explores the theme from the perspective of children of that age. At least one biblical text is explored to help children place the concern within the faith. In the process, children learn appropriate words to use in discussing the theme and while working on the projects. With this background, children select or hear about the projects they will undertake during the year. Each activity in each session concludes with an estimate of the time it will take in parentheses. Some session plans include activities from which you choose the one most appropriate to your class and your time frame.

Possible Projects provides a variety of age-appropriate, hands-on projects related to the theme. They have been chosen to give children firsthand experience with the church's work around that theme and to encourage them to continue to be involved in that concern beyond the class's projects. The list is really a starter list. Some of the projects on it will not be doable in your area. Once you are sure a project is truly "undoable" and not merely "challenging," scratch it off the list. Other projects may call to mind similar efforts that are unique to your area or congregation. Add them to the list. Talk to the mission leaders of your congregation about what your congregation is doing related to this theme and how the children might be involved. Add those possibilities to the list. Connecting to congregational efforts in this way helps the children see themselves as full participants in the congregation's important work. The last item on each project list is a reminder that the most effective projects are those the children suggest and projects they adapt from those on the list. When a class acts on its own ideas and suggestions, the children are empowered and grow to see themselves as capable of loving other people in effective ways. So take the time to involve them as much as possible in choosing and planning the projects.

One practicality: If money is collected for a project, count it together, display a charted record of the growing total, and send it off as a class. Of course, don't mail cash. Also, protect it. Money left in church school class closets often "disappears." So, have one teacher take the collection box home each week, or start a class savings account in which a teacher deposits the money each week and then shows the class the growing record in the savings book.

Fill-In Activities for during the Year are short activities that can be used throughout the year to explore specific pieces of the theme and to keep awareness of the theme alive in the class. They include storybooks to be read and discussed, short games, and simple art activities. Some are seasonal.

These fillers may be scheduled for Sundays on which other activities affect class time. Or they can be used any time a class has a few extra minutes at the end of a session. Or they can be used by a substitute teacher on short notice. A few themes include activities that could be repeated every week of the year. At the beginning of the year, decide how and when you will use the activities you select for your class.

The Summary Session invites the children to recall what they have done, reflect on it, and raise it up before God in worship they have prepared.

One way for congregations to celebrate and reinforce their children's work is to publish an annual Children's Mission Report in which each class describes what it has done. Such reports can be printed flyers handed out with the Sunday worship bulletin, a feature in the congregation's newsletter, or a page of the congregation's website. These reports build adult understanding of the role of children in your congregation and further empower the children. Directions are given in each Summary Session of ways to prepare the class contribution to such a report.

Resources is another starter list. It includes books, games, websites, and other resources that might be useful during the year. Some of them are used in the session plans or filler activities. Most of these resources are available at online bookstores. Many can be found in public libraries. The longer one works with any of these themes, the more resources are found. One way to keep them available is to create a resource box for each grade. Keep all the resources related to that theme in the box with records of class projects and copies of class reports. Also save in the box a file of pictures and patterns that can be reused on bulletin boards and in displays. Keep each box in the classroom where it is used for easy availability.

Leader Support

Most teachers are busy people with multiple commitments. They do best when they have as much support and direction as possible. At the very least they need a clear vision of what is being attempted, a sense of the congregation's commitment, and an introduction to the particulars of the curriculum. Provide this with a brief introduction and a beginning-of-the-year elementary class teacher's meeting. In the introduction include the following:

- the goals of the curriculum and your congregation as you undertake it
- an overview of the five themes
- review of the sections of each theme (Introductory Session, Possible Projects, and so on) with teachers having the curriculum in hand. Curriculum may be copies of the pages of this book. It is also possible to scan these pages to create computer files that can be added to over the years as teams adapt them for use in your congregation and community. In the latter case, give teachers printed copies of the most current version of their grade's theme.
- a walk through calendar dates already scheduled
- time for individual teams to skim their materials and begin planning for their class

Repeat this introduction at the beginning of each year to get new teachers on board and call experienced teachers to deeper understanding of the curriculum and its place in your congregation.

It is also important to keep in touch with teachers as the year progresses. Unless teachers are reminded of scheduled session and project dates, it is easy for them to forget what has been planned. Inquiries into how projects went and which activities are being tried convince teachers that others in the congregation value what they are doing with the children.

Keep the Parents and Congregation Aware of What Is Going On

Introduce the curriculum in the newsletter and on the website. E-mail parents about upcoming project dates in their child's class. Post online and on hallway bulletin boards pictures of children in action. By doing so, you not only help parents get their children to participate but also you enable parents to continue conversations with their children about what they are doing at church. In addition, you build an expectation in the larger congregation that children are important members of this faith community who are active in the congregation's ministry to others.

A Coordinator Helps

Having one person or pair of people at the helm helps. This person or pair needs to:

- prepare the class boxes
- print the curriculum for each grade
- introduce teachers to the curriculum each year
- remind teachers about set dates for sessions and projects
- hear and record for future use teacher reports about how each part has gone
- publicize what is going on to the congregation
- prepare and plan for distribution of a Children's Mission Report

This job could be done by an educator or minister on staff. But it is also a wonderful opportunity for people who care about children and mission but cannot commit to classroom teaching to keep their baptismal promises to the children of the congregation. Members of choirs that practice during the church school hour, teachers who are in a classroom five days a week and need to be somewhere else on Sunday mornings, people who work on weekends or travel a lot and can't make weekly Sunday morning commitments, and people who see themselves more as organizers than teachers are just a few of the good candidates for this position.

CHAPTER FOUR

First Grade: We Are Responsible for the Animals

"I am putting you in charge of the fish, the birds and all the wild animals." (Genesis 1:28b [GNT])

Introduction

CARING FOR ANIMALS IS A GOOD THEME for first graders. It is very concrete and familiar. Many first graders are beginning to assume responsibility for the care of pets at home. Children who do not have pets still live in a world of stuffed animals and animal stories in books and on CDs. They are interested in animals they encounter at zoos and in the wild and even in the backyard. In short, first graders are "into" animals.

By introducing them to the Genesis assignment of responsibility for animals to all humans and involving them in a variety of activities that implement that responsibility, we enable children to both grasp and actually begin exercising their responsible place in God's world. Doing this with animals prepares them to take similar responsibility with other people.

Possible goals for exploring this theme with first graders:

- to enrich children's appreciation for the importance and the place of animals in God's creation
- to claim our responsibility to not forget animals who depend on us for food, water, exercise, and so on
- to stress the importance of not abusing any animals (not even insects) ever
- to celebrate partnerships between humans and animals, e.g., guide dogs and Heifer gift animals
- to learn how humans thoughtlessly destroy animal habitats and how we can take action to protect animals

Introductory Session

As children arrive, invite them to join in **assembling a jigsaw puzzle** that includes lots of animals. Encourage conversation about those animals as you look together for pieces. Or provide **pictures of many kinds of animals to sort through and discuss**. Pictures may be found in *National Geographic* or in picture books about animals. Both activities can be offered at the same time to larger classes.

Read a storybook of the creation story. *Creation*, by Gerald McDermott, is an especially good choice since it focuses on human responsibility for the creatures. Other good possibilities include James Weldon Johnson's poetic version, *The Creation*, or Leonard Everett Fisher's *Seven Days of Creation*. You may also find good versions in Bible storybooks at home or your church library. (7 minutes)

Help the children find **Genesis 1:26-28** in their Bibles. Read it aloud to them, focusing on the phrase, "I am putting you in charge of the fish, the birds, and all the wild animals." Ask, "I wonder what it means to be in charge of the fish, the birds, and all the wild animals?" To enrich the conversation, present a series of pictures of a variety of animals, asking the group what we can do to "be in charge of" each animal. Choose some wild and some domestic animals. Starting with a dog or cat will help get the conversation going. (8 minutes)

Brainstorm an animal alphabet. Work as a group to think of animals that begin with each letter of the alphabet or work in smaller groups on parts of the alphabet. Then, regather to merge the lists into a whole alphabet. One class named seventy-seven animals. (10 minutes)

After talking about lots of kinds of animals, invite each child to **make one animal with clay**. Use clay that will air-dry during the week. Take time for children to introduce their animals and say one way we take responsibility for each one. As children arrive on the following Sunday, work with them to arrange the dried animals into a display. Children may want to draw a backdrop of rocks and trees and sky. (15 minutes today)

Choose the project as a class or introduce the hands-on project(s) you chose for the year. Identify first steps and explain when work on the project will begin. (5 minutes)

Closing: Read the **Group Echo Reading of Psalm 8**. To prepare, invite each child to think of the sound one animal makes and be ready to make that sound when pointed to by the leader. Also tell them to echo (repeat) everything you do and say in the psalm. After the reading, close with a prayer thanking God for giving us responsibility for the animals and asking God's help to do the job well. (5 minutes)

Psalm 8 Group Echo Reading

(**Bold** words are said with emphasis. Directions for actions are in *italics*.)

O Lord,
our Lord,
your greatness is seen in all the world!
> *Spread arms wide to encompass the earth.*

Your praise reaches up to the heavens;
> *Swing one arm from left to right over your head and look to the sky.*

It is sung by children and babies.
> *Rock a baby in your arms.*

You are safe and secure from all your enemies;
> *Stand straight with your arms crossed over your chest.*

You stop anyone who opposes you.
> *Move both hands up into the stop signal.*

When I look at the sky,
> *Swing your arm from left to right over your head and look to the sky.*

which **you** have made,
> *Point up.*

At the moon (*make a moon with your hands*)
and the stars (*sprinkle stars in the sky with your fingers*),
which **you** set in their places —
> *Point to the sky.*

What are human beings, that you think of them;
> *Throw hands out at your sides and shrug with questioning expression on your face.*

Mere mortals, that you care for them?
> *Fold hands on your chest and maintain questioning expression.*

Yet you made them inferior only to yourself; you crowned them with glory and honor.
> *With your hands make a crown on your head.*

You appointed them **rulers** over everything you made.
You put them **in charge of** everything you made.
You made them **responsible for** everything you made.
You placed them over all creation!

Sheep (*baa*)
and cattle (*moo*),
and the wild animals too (*point to individual children to make one animal sound*);
the birds (*flap your arms like wings*)
and the fish (*swim your hands as if they were fish*)
and the creatures in the seas (*make your hands jump like whales*).

O Lord,
our Lord,
your greatness is seen in all the world!
> *Spread arms wide to encompass the earth.*

(Based on Good News Translation)

From *Raising Children to Love Their Neighbors* by Carolyn Brown. © Abingdon Press, 2008. Reproduced by permission.

Project Possibilities

1. **Collect items needed at the Humane Society:** old towels, sheets, or blankets; cardboard tubes (for animal toys); animal toys; gerbil bedding; newspapers to shred (bedding for larger animals); even dog or cat food. At Christmas, Valentine's Day, or anytime, children can make dog biscuits using the recipe below. Your local animal shelter may send a staff person, perhaps accompanied by a puppy or kitten if you ask, to receive these items and tell the children about the work of the SPCA.

   PET COOKIES

   ### Cheese Bone Cookies

2 cups	all purpose flour
1¼ cup	cheese, any kind, shredded
2	garlic cloves, minced
½ cup	vegetable oil
4 tbsp.	water

   Preheat oven to 400 degrees. Combine flour, cheese, garlic, and oil, knead well. Add water, if needed to form stiff dough. Roll out on floured surface to one-half-inch thick, cut into shapes using cookie cutters. Place on ungreased cookie sheets. Bake 10 to 15 minutes or until bottoms are lightly browned. Cool on wire rack. Refrigerate in airtight container.

2. Because the **cost of training a guide dog and the person the dog serves** is so high, this work is done by nonprofit companies that need financial contributions. Search "seeing eye dogs" on the Internet to learn if there is one near you. If there is not, consider the following. Pennies for Puppies at The Seeing Eye, Inc. (www.seeingeye.org) based in Morristown, New Jersey, raises money for their dogs. The Eye Dog Foundation for the Blind (www.eyedogfoundation.org), based in Arizona, lists a variety of donation possibilities including buying a dog harness and leash for $100. And Guide Dogs of America (www.guidedogsofamerica.org), based in California, offers some items for purchase starting at $25. The last two have lists of books and videos to be ordered. Other books may be available in your public library. One is listed in the Resources section.

3. Devote a class session to **animals with which we live.** Ask children before class to bring pictures of themselves and their pets. Invite children to introduce their pets and talk about how they care for them. Then show pictures of other animals we frequently encounter, such as birds, insects, and small reptiles. Together write a list of rules for taking care of God's animals. Create a bulletin board by posting those rules in the center and pinning all the other photographs of animals around it. The following week give each child a copy of the class rules, perhaps printed on a bookmark.

4. **Buy an animal for Heifer Project**. Their website (www.heifer.org) offers a catalogue of animals at many prices. A goat can be purchased for $120. Two books, *Beatrice's Goat* and *Charlie Needs a Cloak* (both available in many public libraries) explain the value of a goat. Children can make their own goat banks by wrapping the cut-out and colored goat pattern around an empty can. If you use a lidded microwaveable soup container, cut a slit in the lid for coins and tape the goat around the outer rim of the lid. For extra pizzazz glue a yarn tail to the back end of the goat pattern. Fourteen children each raising one dollar a month could buy a goat in a nine-month school year. Keep a chart of your progress (color in sections of the animal) publicly displayed with other information about the chosen animal. From time to time, bring in products provided by your animal, for example, for a goat, taste goat's milk or cheese.

5. Check the website of the zoo nearest you. Most **zoos offer service projects for children**. For example, Zoo Atlanta collects used cell phones for recycling on behalf of gorilla conservation and urges children to recycle aluminum cans so that less forest land will be cleared to mine more aluminum, thus protecting animal habitats. The National Zoo in Washington D.C. invites children to sponsor a panda for $50. In response they send a plush panda and a kit of information about pandas.

Remember that the highest-impact projects are those the children choose or shape themselves. These projects empower them. They teach them that they can make a difference in the world. So be responsive to their ideas about shaping these projects and alert to their ideas for other projects. The best project for the year may not be on this list!

Fill-In Activities for during the Year

1. **Maintain a bulletin board throughout the year with pictures of animals and people caring for them.** Invite children to bring pictures from magazines and newspapers or their own drawings or photographs of animals. Stay alert for news stories involving animals—especially those that encourage responsible treatment of animals.

2. **Make doorknob hangers** with the message, "Let us take care of God's animals." Copy the pattern onto stiff paper or card stock for children to cut out and color. Hang them on doorknobs around the church and encourage the children to hang them on their doorknobs at home.

3. **Read and discuss a poem** from *God Listens to Your Care: Prayers for All the Animals of the World*. Read through each poem before reading it with children to be sure you are ready to explore its topic with your children at this time.

4. **Play "Mother May I," giving permission to take animal-type steps** forward, for example, one kangaroo hop (two-footed hop), two crab steps (holding ankles with hands), one inchworm step (put hands on floor in front of you and walk feet up to them), and so on.

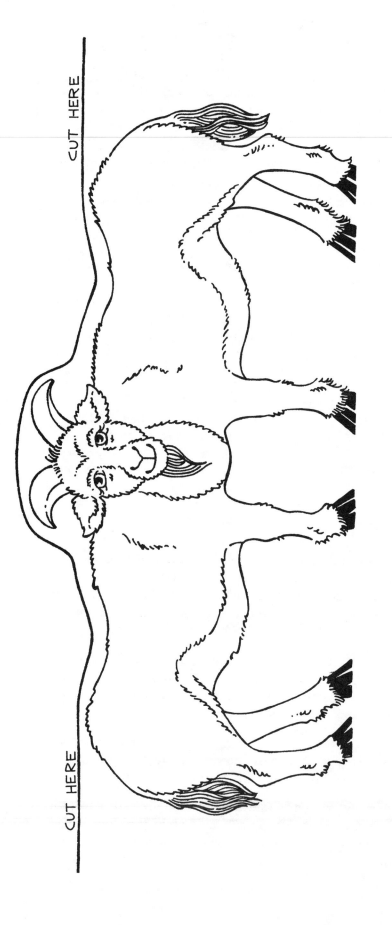

CUT HERE

CUT HERE

Let us take care
of God's Animals

5. **Play games with a collection of small plastic animals.**
   - All players hide their eyes while the whole collection is hidden around the room. Players then either search for the animals until all are found or look for the animals from their seats, raising a hand when they see one. When recognized by the leader, the seated player goes to claim the animal.
   - Before class a teacher hides only one animal in an inconspicuous, but visible place. At some point during the class, the teacher says, "I am thinking of an animal that . . ." and gives a series of clues about the animal. Children listen to the clues and look around the room for the animal. When they both know the animal and can point to it, they raise their hand. If other children are still looking, the teacher may invite those "in the know" to offer clues. After they get the hang of the game, children can take turns selecting the animal, hiding it, and giving the clues.

6. Read God's dream for a new day in **Isaiah 11:6-9**. Note the animals that will get along with other animals with which they are now enemies. Sort a pile of animal pictures into pairs that do and do not get along. Play with new pairings in which animals that do not get along live together in peace, such as the lion and the lamb.

7. During Advent, make **a nativity mural with lots of animals in it**. Before class, post a nativity scene with the basic people already drawn in place. With the children, make a list of the animals that need to be added. To complete your list, read *The Friendly Beasts*, Tomie dePaola's illustration of the familiar carol, and *We Were There*, which tells of the loving presence of often overlooked animals, such as bat, cockroach, and rat. Then help children make the animals out of textured papers, cloths, and yarns to add to the manger scene. Conclude with prayer, thanking God for including animals at Christmas.

Summary Session

Begin with the activities with which you started the introductory session. Invite early arrivers to work on the animal jigsaw puzzle with you, talking about animals as you work. When all have arrived, read the creation story you read to start the first session. Then help the children look up Genesis 1:26 and read it again. (20 minutes)

Together make a list of ways you have exercised your responsibility for animals this year. Celebrate your hands-on projects. With a teacher as scribe, **work together on composing a paragraph describing what you did for the congregation's newsletter or website or for a children's mission flyer.** Invite children to draw pictures of what you did to be used with their report. Dedicate your efforts to God in prayer together. (10 minutes)

If you have time, do the following or select an activity from the filler list, possibly one you have done before as a class and especially enjoyed.

Create and illustrate prayers for or about specific animals. To get started read one or two animal prayers from *Prayers from the Ark*, inviting children to guess which animal prays each prayer. The prayers of the little ducks, the donkey, the monkey, and the mouse are among the easiest for first graders to understand. Post the children's illustrated prayers on a class or hallway bulletin board. (15 minutes)

For your closing worship, ask each child to say his or her prayer. After each prayer, the whole class adds, "God, help us take care of the animals." Or repeat the Echo Reading of Psalm 8 from the introductory session. (5 minutes)

Resources

Androcles and the Lion
   There are many versions of this old fable about a runaway slave who pulls a thorn out of a lion's paw and then is saved by the lion who recognizes him when they are thrown together in the Roman coliseum. Find a copy at your local library or bookstore.

Beatrice's Goat, Paige McBrier (New York: Atheneum, 2001).
   The story of all the positive changes that come to a young girl in Africa when her family receives a Heifer Project goat.

Charlie Needs a Cloak, Tomie DePaola (New York: Simon and Schuster, 1974).
   The story of all the work needed as a ragged shepherd makes a new cloak for himself.

The Creation, James Weldon Johnson (Holiday House, 1995).
   Poem describing God's creation of the world in the voice of an African American grandparent telling the story. Beautiful word images convey the meaning of the story.

Creation, Gerald McDermott (New York: Dutton, 2003).
   This beautifully illustrated, simply worded account of creation roughly follows Genesis 1. It focuses on the care of the creatures with which man and woman are entrusted. This is a book to savor with children. After reading through it once to get the story and learn the ending, take time to identify the creatures in the art, to say how each is a gift, and how we can take care of them. It is a good book to use with a group or just to have around for a child to enjoy alone.

The Friendly Beasts, illustrated by Sharon McGinley (Greenwillow Books, 2000) or
The Friendly Beasts, illustrated by Tomie dePaola (New York: Putnam, 1981).
   Beautiful illustrations of the verses of this familiar children's Christmas carol describing the gifts a variety of animals offered the baby Jesus. Children who know the song may prefer to sing rather than read the text during Advent, perhaps during a class Christmas party.

The Goat Lady, by Jane Bregoli (Gardiner, Maine: Tilbury House, 2004).
A gentle story of the partnership between an old lady and her goats and the way a family helps her be accepted in their community. Pair it with *Beatrice's Goat* to hear about goats who were sent to Heifer Project as well as a family that received a goat.

God Listens to Your Care: Prayers for All the Animals of the World, Carol J. Adams (Cleveland, Ohio: Pilgrim Press, 2006).
A collection of prayer poems voiced by animals about their concerns. Many are good discussion starters or "write a prayer for an animal" starters. Do pre-read these prayers as some deal with subjects such as death or the use of animals that you may or may not want to discuss with the children.

I Sing for the Animals, Paul Goble (New York: Simon and Schuster, 1991).
A small book that comes from an American Indian background about our relationship with the animals. Beautiful art.

Looking Out for Sarah, Glenna Lang (Watertown, Mass.: Charlesbridge, 2001).
Follow a seeing eye dog and the dog's blind companion through a day together to learn how they work as a team.

"Partners" and "Adam's Animals," from *Does God Have A Big Toe*, Marc Gellman (New York: Harper Collins, 1989).
Two stories from a collection: "Partners" tells how God made Adam and Eve partners in caring for the created world. In "Adam's Animals," Adam makes humorous attempts at naming the animals before letting the animals tell him their names.

Prayers from the Ark, Carmen Bernos De Gasztold (New York: Viking, 1962; Puffin Reprint Editions, 1995).
Select from this collection of poetic prayers of the animals on the ark the prayers that children understand. The imagery and ideas in some of the prayers are beyond the understanding of first graders.

Seven Days of Creation, Leonard Everett Fisher (New York: Holiday House, 1981).
A simple, well-illustrated retelling of the Genesis 1 creation story.

Song of Creation, Paul Goble (Grand Rapids: Eerdmans, 2004).
This is a beautiful illustration and amplification of a prayer from *The Book of Common Prayer* calling all parts of creation to praise God. The author/illustrator prints the words from the prayer book prayer in large print, then adds specific versions of the prayer for specific animals in smaller print, all illustrated in art bearing the flavor of the Southwest.

We Were There, by Eve Bunting (New York: Clarion Books, 2001).
The story of seven animals who were there unnoticed at the Nativity—a snake, a toad, a scorpion, a cockroach, a bat, a spider, and a rat who slept in the stable during the day and ate crumbs in the inn at night. This is a challenge for children to think about all the animals who might have been present in the stable when Jesus was born.

CHAPTER FIVE

Second Grade: Sharing So Every Body Has Enough

"I was hungry and you gave me food,
I was thirsty and you gave me something to drink . . .
I was naked and you gave me clothing,
I was sick and you took care of me." (Matthew 25:35-36)

Introduction

SECOND GRADERS ARE VERY AWARE OF THEIR BODIES. Most are happily able to use their bodies to master more and more tasks and sports. All are learning about their bodies in science and health classes. So, it is a good year to link their interest in their bodies to an awareness of the needs of bodies other than their own. Every body needs water, food, clothes, and medicine. One way we respond to Jesus' command, "Love one another" is to be sure our neighbors' bodies have what they need. So this year, second graders are invited to learn about some ways people have worked to provide for the physical needs of others and to participate in at least two projects in which they meet the physical needs of others.

Compassion and *sharing* are the key words underlying all the activities of the year. Compassion means learning to watch for the needs of others and to do what we can to ease them. Sharing means giving others some of what we have so that all may have enough. Both are tough sells in our culture, especially for children. Children are encouraged to focus on individual achievement and to protect themselves from, rather than care for, other people, particularly those they do not know. Stories of compassionate heroes and heroines offer an alternative vision, even the seeds for future vocations.

Possible Goals for Exploring This Theme with Second Graders:

- to encourage children to look beyond their own needs to the needs of those around them

- to explore with the children the difficulties some people have getting water, food, clothes, and medicine
- to introduce children to at least two ways the church has worked to meet the needs of bodies all around the world
- to help children recognize themselves as people who can help others in need

Introductory Session

Before class, draw a body outline and "Bodies Need" title on a **bulletin board**. (Think a very large gingerbread man or stick figure.) As a class, brainstorm different physical needs every body has (water, food, clothing, medicine, and maybe other things the children will suggest). Write these needs in large print around the body. Then, talk about what happens when a body does not get each of these. Write key words describing these needs in a different color near each item, such as hunger and starvation near "food." Add pictures of people who are facing these needs. *National Geographic* is a good source of such pictures. (10 minutes)

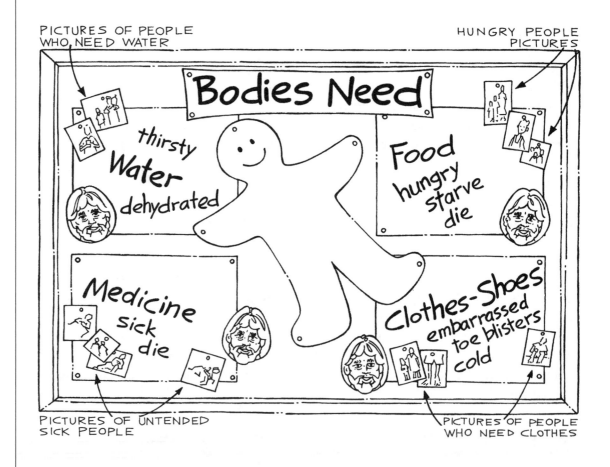

From *Raising Children to Love Their Neighbors* by Carolyn Brown. © Abingdon Press, 2008. Reproduced by permission.

Help the children find Matthew 25:35-40 in their Bibles. Read it aloud as they follow along. Discuss what Jesus was telling us. At the end of your discussion, place pictures of Jesus' face around or near the pictures of the people in need on the bulletin board as a reminder to see in each person the face of Jesus. (10 minutes)

To learn how at least one person has met the needs of others, **start reading one of the books about a compassionate hero or heroine** from the bibliography. (Some of the longer books will need to be read over several weeks.) (10 minutes)

Do a sharing exercise. Divide the class into small groups, perhaps seated at separate tables. Give one group a bottle of juice, another a set of cups, another a bag of crackers or cookies, and another napkins. Tell them to enjoy their snack. Step back as long as seems wise to see what the children will do. If they do not start working out a plan for sharing, ask leading questions suggesting possibilities for sharing. Keep the tone light and enjoy your snack together. But at some point, refer to your bulletin board. Note that just as your class had plenty to go around for snack, we have plenty of food and water in the world. But, just as it was not easy to figure out how to share our snack, sometimes it is not easy to find ways to be sure every body has the water, food, clothes, and medicine it needs. Present this difficulty as a worthy challenge as the class works on its projects this year. (10 minutes)

Introduce the chosen projects or decide as a class the first project you will undertake together to follow Jesus' command. Select from the list of projects or other mission work of your congregation. (7 minutes)

To close the session, read the great commands from Mark 12:28-31 to the children and offer prayer asking God to be with you as you work this year on your particular projects to take care of bodies. (3 minutes)

Project Possibilities

1. Many denominations collect a congregation-wide offering during Lent for hunger and relief missions. For many it is called **One Great Hour of Sharing**. Prepared materials for these offerings often include coin boxes, games, and educational flyers for children. If your congregation participates in such an offering, second grade is a good year to emphasize it with children. Having explored the offering's purpose early in their elementary years, they will participate readily and with quick understanding in later years. There are many ways to work with them.

   Send a letter to parents as the offering is introduced, explaining its place in the second-grade curriculum. Encourage families to give it regular attention by keeping the coin box/es in a prominent place and adding coins regularly. If a calendar with daily contribution activities ("give five cents for each blanket in the house") is included, mention it and encourage its regular use as a way for parents to talk with their children about their care for other people in the world.

   Take time each week in class to use some of the educational materials to explore the work supported by the offering and to encourage children to participate at home.

   Involve the children in promoting the offering to other children or the whole congregation by helping them post preprinted materials around the church building, making announcements about it to other children's classes, even presenting a minute for mission about it during the congregation's worship.

   Together count the coin box offerings of your class. Divide into several groups to open and count a small number of boxes. Write small group totals on the board to add up for the class total. Dedicate in prayer your offering to people who have needs. Ask God to watch over the offering's use. Together deliver it to the appropriate place.

2. Most **community food banks** have a list of the food that goes into an emergency food box for a family. As a class, fill at least one box. Either ask each child to bring a preset money contribution, then go together to a grocery store and gather the items on the list, or divide the list among the children, assigning each child one or more items to bring. Then pack the box as a group. If possible, deliver your box to the food bank together. If that is not possible, send a camera with those who make the delivery (hopefully including a few second graders) and get a picture to illustrate your report to the children.

3. **Trick or Treat for UNICEF,** collecting money to meet the physical needs of people around the world. Send the children out to collect on Halloween. Or plan for them to wear their costumes to church on the Sunday before or after Halloween. Send one or two children to stand at each sanctuary door at the close of the service to collect coins from departing worshipers. If you choose the latter, check with the appropriate church committees for permission. No matter how you collect the money, bring it back and count it together. Celebrate whatever sum the class raised and what might be done with it. Visit www.unicef.org on your own or with the children to find details about the Trick or Treat campaign, to learn about the work of UNICEF, and to read the stories of other children who support its work.

4. **Go to www.churchworldservice.org,** click on the "Build a Village" icon, then on "Give a Gift" icon. Here you find opportunities to help—many are within the financial range of a second-grade class (Health Kits, School Kits, Clean Up after a Disaster Kits, and others). As you make your selection, remember that the children did projects related to animals in first grade and that they will do projects related to homelessness, including buying blankets for people caught in disasters, in third grade. Therefore, it is best to choose other kinds of projects for this year. (Church World Service is the relief, development, and refugee assistance ministry of thirty-five Protestant, Orthodox, and Anglican denominations in the United States. Working in partnership with indigenous organizations in more than eighty countries, CWS works worldwide to meet human needs and foster self-reliance for all whose way is hard.)

5. If your community sponsors a **CROP Walk** or other hunger walk, walk the first three miles. Before walking, collect contributions. If the walk is on a Sunday, encourage children to wear walking clothes to church and collect sponsorships at a booth at a busy place in the church building. Again, total your collections before turning them in, talk about what can be done with that much money, and dedicate it in prayer to hungry people.

6. **Cook a meal at a soup kitchen or shelter.** Many community shelters rely on congregations to provide teams for this "not as scary as it sounds at first" ministry. Some groups provide menus with simple recipes and most have staff on duty to work with you. Larger classes may need to divide into two or more groups. It is also a great activity in which to include families. Important conversations about the experience often take place in the car on the way home.

7. **Participate as a class in collections sponsored by local clubs,** e.g., collect eyeglasses from your congregation for the local Lions Clubs for distribution in developing countries, collect new socks for a local clothing bank, and so on. Ask the chair of your congregation's mission committee to pass on needs of local groups with which your congregation works.

8. **If there is a high-profile natural disaster during the year,** second graders will often want to do something to respond. Recent disasters have taught the futility of well-meaning individuals trucking lots of stuff into the affected area. National groups now preorganize for the collection and distribution of health kits, school supply kits, and more. Check your denomination's website. If there is nothing there, go to www.churchworldservice.org to find a list of kits needed, assemble several kits, and earmark them for the affected area.

Remember that the highest-impact projects are those the children choose or shape themselves. These projects empower them. They teach them that they can make a difference in the world. So be responsive to their ideas about shaping these projects and alert to their ideas for other projects. The best project for the year may not be on this list!

Fill-In Activities for during the Year

1. **Maintain a bulletin board about people with "body" needs.** Watch for accounts about both people with needs and people who meet needs. Clip pictures from newspapers and magazines and encourage children to do the same. Talk and pray together about people who catch the children's interest.

2. **Go to www.churchworldservice.org** and click on the "Build a Village" icon to find a collection of **quizzes, word searches, even jigsaw puzzles** with which to explore use of water, food, and so forth around the world. All of these, except the jigsaw puzzles, can be either printed or used online. These activities cover water, food, medical care, and help in times of trouble.

3. **As a class, make a list of all the ways you use water in one day.** Guess how much water that is. Discuss how it came to you, through wells or city water systems. Wonder what it would be like if you had to carry every drop of what you use from a source a mile from your house. Who would do the carrying? How long would it take to get it? Which of your current uses would you have to give up?

4. **Play games carrying gallon milk jugs filled with water.** Give each child a jug to carry all around the church property or to a destination down the street and back. Then do the activities in no. 3. Or, in teams do relay races, carrying water jugs to a goal and back to the next teammate. The point is to get a feel for how heavy water is and thus to begin imagining what it would be like to have to carry all the water your family uses from a distant source. Just for fun after the race, sit down for a rest and a cup of water. Read from a Bible storybook

or tell in your own words the story of Rebekah, who offered to draw water for ten camels (Gen. 24). Imagine how much water ten camels could drink and how much work it would be to draw that from a well. That's compassion!

5. **If one of the second graders breaks a bone, has a similar medical emergency, or has a baby born into the family during the year,** interview him or her with the class about the medical response. Who helped? What equipment did they use? What tests were made? What labs and/or clinics did the child visit? Lead the class to imagine what might have happened had some of these people and services not been available.

6. **Invite a church member who has been on a mission trip focused on meeting physical needs to speak to the class.** Ask them to describe the need, how they worked to meet it, and how life was different for people after they left. (Save speakers who have built houses on their mission trips for the fourth-grade emphasis on homelessness.)

7. **Interview a person whose career involves getting people the things they need.** Look for medical personnel who work at free clinics, public health nurses, someone who works at the community food bank, and so forth. If possible, choose a member of your congregation.

8. During Advent **read and discuss** *Why the Chimes Rang* (see Resources).

9. Invite the children to **make a table tent bearing two mealtime blessings** for their tables at home. Copy the pattern on the next page onto stiff paper. The mealtime blessing printed on it raises concern for those who do not have food. Read that blessing and discuss it, raising the possibility of remembering people all around the world eating every time we sit down to eat. Then suggest that children print another blessing they know on the other side of the tent. Decorate both sides with student-drawn food and cooking utensil pictures. Finally fold along the dotted lines and staple into a freestanding tent.

_____

_____

_____

_____

_____

_____

_____

_____

_____

Nicaraguan Prayer

O God,
Bless this food we are about to receive.
Give bread to those who hunger,
and give hunger for justice
to us who have bread.

Summary Session

Before class, make a pallet on which to carry a paralyzed man to be healed by Jesus. Seal a three-cubic-yard sack of mulch into a heavy duty garbage bag with wrapping tape. Create carrying handles near the corners by wrapping packing tape several times around the bag, leaving big loops on either side. Press the sides of the loops together to form straps/handles. See illustration. (Four children, one at each handle, will have to work together to carry this pallet on level ground and work even harder to get it up a flight of stairs.) Also, cut out a very large paper gingerbread person shape to lie on the "pallet."

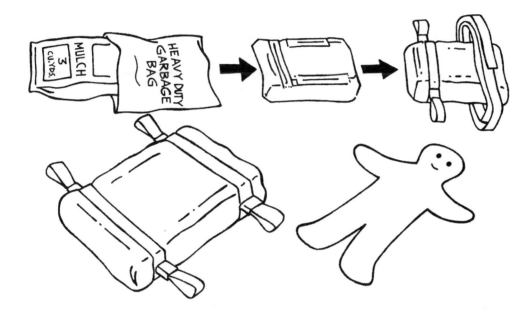

As children arrive, have them work on coloring in the paper figure of the paralyzed man and then have them lay it on the top of the pallet.

Read or tell the biblical story "Four Friends Work for a Healing." See next page. (5 minutes)

Four Friends Work for a Healing
(Based on Luke 5:17-26)

When Jesus was in Capernaum, large crowds followed him everywhere. One day he was teaching in a house. People were not only packed as tightly into the house as they could be but also they filled the yard listening through the open windows and doors. Four men arrived in the yard carrying their paralyzed friend on a mat. With such a crowd, there was no way they could get close to Jesus. But one of them had an idea!

They gently carried their friend up the outside steps to the roof of the house, then carefully opened a hole in the roof and lowered their friend on his mat directly in front of Jesus. Everyone stepped back to make room. Jesus looked down at the man on the mat and up at the friends looking through the roof.

"What great faith you have!" he said to the friends.

Then to the man on the pallet Jesus said, "Get up. Take your mat and go home."

The man slowly moved his hands and feet. Cautiously, he sat up. Then he stood. Then, with a huge smile, he bent down, rolled up his mat and walked through the crowd toward the door. There was a happy roar from the crowd as his friends joined him and they ran happily down the road together.

Do the following to explore the story.

Lead the children in imagining what it would be like to be paralyzed. If there is room, ask them to lie on their backs on the floor. If there is not room, ask them to sit with hands in their laps in their chairs. Tell them they are paralyzed and ask them to imagine such situations as your nose itches, you are hungry, you are thirsty, you have been left lying in the sun and are getting hot, you hear something fall and break somewhere in the house, you hear people laughing and talking in the street, and so on. After "unparalyzing" them, discuss the frustrations and wonder what life had been like for the paralyzed man on the pallet. (5 minutes)

To satisfy curiosity about how the friends could make a hole in the roof, describe how roofs were constructed in those days. Palm branches were laid across long wooden sticks that were laid across beams. There is a useful picture on page 216 of *The Illustrated Children's Bible*. You may find other good pictures in teaching-pictures files at your church or in Bible storybooks.

Take turns carrying the mulch pallet up and down a flight of steps to see how hard it was to get a man up the stairs to the roof. Encourage the children to imagine that the paper figure is a real person who could fall off. (10 minutes)

Finally reread or retell the story. Direct attention to Jesus' compliment to the friends, "What great faith you have!" What was he complimenting them on?

Review what you have done this year on this mission theme (put out materials, samples, thank-you notes, and so on from the year's work). Ask which were the hard parts of these projects. Point out the ways the children kept working past the challenges and compare them to the four friends who kept working past their challenges to get the man on the pallet healed. Talk about the challenges people face trying to get assistance to those caught in disasters and compare them to the four friends. Celebrate all this faithful perseverance. (10 minutes)

If there is going to be a children's report or pamphlet about their mission projects this year, plan your contribution together. Write on a chalkboard several student-dictated sentences describing each project. Ask the group to evaluate their work with such questions as "What have you learned since we made our first bulletin board this fall?" and "What else would you like to do about this?" Edit your sentences until the group is satisfied. If you took photos of the class's work, select one or two to illustrate the statement. (15 minutes)

If there will not be a children's printed report, as a class **create a bulletin board of what you have done.** If the original bulletin board is still up, add pictures of and materials from your work near the "body needs each" project addresses. Or create a fresh bulletin board by drawing a large gingerbread person in the center. With the children add words and pictures that describe the body needs your group addressed. Add materials related to your project, including photos, coin boxes, and the amounts of money raised or things collected. (15 minutes)

To **create a litany celebrating your mission work this year,** begin by rereading Matthew 25:34-40. Then work with the children to rephrase the biblical words into words related to your projects. For example:

Teacher:	We saw people in Africa without water.
Students:	So we collected money for a well pump.
All:	Jesus, we did it for them but we also did it for you.
Teacher:	We saw hungry people in (your town).
Students:	So we took food for them to the food bank.
All:	Jesus, we did it for them but we also did it for you.

(7 minutes)

Together **write a prayer** telling God about what you have done and asking for help finding ways to take care of all bodies everywhere. (7 minutes)

Close by standing facing your project bulletin board or around a table featuring items from your projects to recite the litany and pray the prayer you have written for these projects. (3 minutes)

Resources

A Rose for Abby, Donna Guthrie (Nashville: Abingdon Press, 1988, 1998).
A young girl watches an elderly street woman digging through the trash cans near her church and decides to do something to help out. A simple story about finding simple ways to alleviate the suffering of people around us.

Florence Nightingale, War Nurse, by Anne Colver (New York: Chelsea House, 1961).
A chapter book biography of the woman whose love of caring for others led her to found the modern nursing career. Read and discuss a chapter or two each week for a month or two.

Joseph: King of Dreams, animated full length DVD.
Click on Selected Scenes then start with no. 13, "Joseph Meets Pharoah." Watch the section about Joseph interpreting Pharoah's dreams, handling the storage of food during the good years, and distributing grain during the famine. Stop when a little girl drops her doll as Joseph's brothers appear in line. Children will need some help identifying what Joseph did to help people get through the famine and comparing what Joseph did with what people do today to deliver food to people after natural disasters.

Stone Soup, Jon J Muth (New York: Scholastic, 2003).
An old story about hungry strangers who lead an ungenerous village into feeding them by drawing them into making a large pot of "stone soup" for the whole village. This version of the tale is set in China with monks as the strangers. It is beautifully illustrated and very clear that sharing what we have leads to happiness for everyone.

Uncle Willie and the Soup Kitchen, DyAnne Disalvo-Ryan (New York: Morrow, 1991, Harper Trophy Reprint, 1997).
A young boy spends the day with his uncle gathering food and preparing it at a soup kitchen. Read this book before working at a soup kitchen or simply as a discussion starter about sharing food with others.

Why the Chimes Rang, Raymond MacDonald Alden (Emmis Books, Guild Press of Indiana, 2006).
In this 2006 release of a 1909 classic, the coin given to a little boy by his brother who gave up the trip to the great cathedral on Christmas Eve to take care of an old woman dying in the snow causes the cathedral chimes to ring. Other magnificent gifts given out of the abundance of the givers did not do so.

CHAPTER SIX

Third Grade: It Is a Global Neighborhood

"Let us love one another, because love comes from God." (1 John 4:7 [GNT])

Introduction

"Love the Lord your God with all your heart, with all your soul, and with all your mind." (Matt. 22:37 [GNT])

"Love your neighbor as you love yourself." (Matt. 22:39 [GNT])

"Let us love one another, because love comes from God." (1 John 4:7 [GNT])

"If we say we love God, but hate others, we are liars." (1 John 4:20 [GNT])

"So then, show love for those foreigners, because you were once foreigners in Egypt." (Deut. 10:19 [GNT])

Scriptures repeatedly make it clear that we are meant to live together in harmony. It is not an option to be tried, but rather an obligation at the very core of our existence. In today's world the norm is to be fearful of people "not like us" and hence to know, love, and work with only those who are "like us." In the United States, it is easy to fear that any Middle Eastern person may be a terrorist. Each race fears the other races will mistreat them. The "circle the wagons" mentality, ignoring all but our own people, can become our default position. In such a world, if we want our children to love their neighbors as they love themselves and to form good working partnerships with people who are different, we must intentionally lead them to do that. So this year's mission theme is devoted to building bridges between people who are different.

There are several challenges. One is to alert the children to the many different ways people live and do things and to find those differences interesting rather than threatening.

Hopefully, this is not a new idea to third graders and the year's classroom activities will be reinforcing a familiar attitude. A second challenge is to begin identifying those who are outsiders in their own schools and community. Sensitive discussions help children do that. Once these outsiders are identified, it is important to explore ways we can welcome them and see that they are treated well. At that point the children need to actually meet and welcome some people who are different. Those experiences will be harder for the adults to set up because they will most likely require us to move out of our comfort zones too. But these real-life experiences will reap benefits that cannot come from just talking and reading in the classroom.

Possible goals for exploring this theme with third graders:
- to experience differences among people as interesting rather than threatening
- to become more aware of those who are different and how they are treated
- to engage in welcoming at least one different person to learn how it can be done
- to see oneself as a person who can welcome people who are different

Introductory Session

To get started: Help children look up 1 John 4:7 and 1 John 4:20. Read them aloud. Ask the children what these verses mean. Title a bulletin board "Let us love one another," either pinning a preprinted title in place or getting the children to add the precut letters on the board in the proper sequence. (10 minutes)

Explore two biblical stories about being good neighbors. To emphasize the difference in the stories, do each one in a different corner of the room or with the children facing different directions.

1. *Explore Jesus' story about the good Samaritan.* Before reading the story, introduce the words *Samaritan*, *priest*, and *Levite*. If you have a map of New Testament Palestine, point out Samaria.

   Levites were Temple leaders. They were greatly respected by other Jews.

   The priest was responsible for leading worship at the Temple and was also respected.

   Samaritans and Jews lived near each other but hated and distrusted each other. Jews tried to avoid walking through Samaria and would not eat from plates Samaritans had used.

   Involve the children in reading the story, using the script "The Good Neighbor." To make the reading easier, make eight copies before class, highlighting one reader's part on each copy.

   After reading ask:
   - What was Jesus telling the teacher about who his neighbor was?
   - What was Jesus saying about how we treat neighbors?

   (15 minutes)

The Good Neighbor
(Based on Luke 10:25-37)

Leader: A teacher of the Law asked Jesus this question.

Reader 1: Teacher, what must I do to receive eternal life?

Reader 2: What do the scriptures say?

Reader 1: "Love the Lord your God with all your heart, with all your soul, with all your strength, and with all your mind" and "Love your neighbor as you love yourself."

Reader 2: You are right! Do this and you will live.

Reader 1: But who is my neighbor?

Leader: Jesus answered by telling a story.

Reader 3: There was once a man who was going down the road from Jerusalem to Jericho. Robbers attacked him and beat him up. They left him half dead by the side of the road.

Reader 4: A priest came down that road. But when he saw the man, he walked by on the other side.

Reader 5: A Levite also came by. He went over, looked at the man, and then walked by on the other side.

Reader 6: But a Samaritan who was traveling that way also saw the man. He felt sorry for him. He went over to him and bandaged his wounds. Then he put the man on his own animal and took him to an inn, where he took care of him.

Reader 7: The next day he gave the innkeeper two silver coins. The Samaritan told the innkeeper to take care of the man and promised to pay whatever he spent on the victim when he returned.

Leader: Jesus then asked the teacher of the Law,

Reader 2: Which one of the three people acted like a neighbor to the man attacked by robbers?

Reader 1: The one who was kind to him.

Reader 2: You should go do the same thing.

From *Raising Children to Love Their Neighbors* by Carolyn Brown. © Abingdon Press, 2008. Reproduced by permission.

2. *Explore Jonah's story.* Move the group to another part of the room or turn them to face another direction to hear this story, using one of the two activities below.

- If your students are good readers, have them read the story aloud directly from the Bible. (The entire book of Jonah is two pages long in the Good News Bible.) Have students each read one paragraph rather than one verse. At the end of each chapter, pause to be sure everyone knows what has happened so far. (Before going to the discussion questions, celebrate reading an entire book of the Bible together!)
- Read *Jonah and the Whale (and the Worm)* by Jean Marzollo. As you work through the book as a class, read and ponder together all the background comments in the margins and enjoy the humorous comments of the octopi at the bottom of each page. There is one problem with this otherwise wonderful book. The biblical story is open-ended. We do not know if Jonah ever recognized the Ninevites as his neighbors and as worthy of God's forgiveness. Jean Marzollo has decided that Jonah finally did get it and offers that as the ending. To keep with the biblical account, cut out the last page of the book. If students notice that the page is missing, explain the situation and then challenge them to decide whether Jonah finally came around.

After either reading ask:
- Who were Jonah's neighbors?
- How did Jonah feel about his neighbors at the beginning?
- What did God try to teach Jonah about his neighbors?
- Do you think Jonah learned the lesson?
- What was the same and different about Jonah and the Good Samaritan?

(15 minutes)

Show a series of magazine or newspaper pictures of people who look "different," asking the children, "Is this a neighbor?" and discussing why it is easy to be surprised that this person is a neighbor who deserves our friendship. Select pictures of people from different parts of the world and people of different races, dress styles, and so on, whom the children might encounter any day. Post the pictures around the edges of your "Love One Another" bulletin board. (*Portraits* listed in the Resource section is one excellent source.) (10 minutes)

Introduce or choose projects to work on during the coming year. (5 minutes)

Start a "Praying for the World" map. Place a world map in the middle of your "Love One Another" bulletin board. Ask the children which countries their families come from and which countries they have visited. Mark these countries with colored push-pins. Explain that each week this year you will pray for the people in one country. It may be a country that has been in the news. Or it may be a country you have chosen at random. Your goal will be to cover the world with your prayers. Start today by selecting as the recipients for your first prayers the people of a country that has been the focus of your discussions or for people of the United States. As a class, identify some of the things you want to say to God about the selected people. Then one teacher offers these prayers aloud on behalf of the group to close the class. See Filler Activities for ideas about how to continue this project. (5 minutes)

Give each child a globe token. Globes are available as rubber marbles, stickers, backpack tags, or other knickknacks at toy stores, religious book stores, and school supply stores. They can also be ordered from www.ustoy.com or www.oriental trading.com. Give each child one token to carry or display prominently this year as a reminder that they are neighbors to everyone in every place on the globe. Check in occasionally during the year to see if the tokens are still around and what the children think about each time they see or touch theirs.

Project Possibilities

Before you choose your projects, find out which projects your children did as second graders to provide for the physical needs of others. A few projects listed below were also offered for second grade. To give the children as many different experiences as possible, it is best to choose different projects for each year.

1. The first Sunday in October is **World Communion Sunday**. Christians in all denominations celebrate the Lord's Supper on this day. Breads from all nations (Russian pumpernickel, pita bread, sourdough bread, corn bread, and tortillas) are used on this day. Offer for the third graders to prepare a display of such breads in a large basket for the front of the sanctuary, perhaps taking the place of flowers. Or offer to provide a variety of cubed breads ready for use in Communion that day. It is easier for children to cut bread cubes if the breads are presliced and frozen. For safety, seat children around tables with individual cutting boards and plenty of work space. Cut bread a week early and store the cubes in plastic bags in the freezer. They thaw quickly when poured into baskets before the service.

2. **Trick or Treat for UNICEF,** collecting money to meet the needs of people around the world. Send the children out to collect on Halloween. Or plan for them to wear their costumes to church on the Sunday before or after Halloween. Send one or two children to stand at each sanctuary door at the close of the service to collect from departing worshipers. If you choose the latter, check with the appropriate church committees for permission. No matter how you collect the money, bring it back and count it together. Celebrate whatever sum the class raised and what might be done with it. Visit www.unicef.org on your own or with the children to find details about the Trick or Treat campaign, to learn about the work of UNICEF, and to read the stories of other children who support its work.

3. **Invite an immigrant** (if possible, a member of the congregation) to tell the children about his or her move. Ask the person to describe what is the same and what is different about life in their former home and their new home. Also ask what was hard about moving and what people in the United States did to welcome them that was especially helpful.

4. **Befriend an international student as a class** by doing some of the following. (Find international student connections by contacting a local college or looking under "International" in the business section of your telephone book.)
   * Invite the student to visit your class. Spend some time hearing about the student's home country and some time telling him or her about your lives. Plan for some children to accompany the student to worship and even have lunch together at the church following worship. Take pictures to post around the room for the year.
   * Keep stationery and stamps in the room to send messages throughout the year.
   * Invite the student to a Christmas event at your church and plan a way to talk with the student about Christmas (or a similar holiday) at their home and here.
   * Make Valentine's Day cards and birthday cards for the student.

5. If there is a **Christmas International House** in your town, as a class offer to host a children's games party for the students one afternoon or evening during the Christmas break. The class could provide Christmas cookies and punch as refreshments, teach a few U.S. children's games, and learn from the students games that children play in their countries. To learn if Christmas International House is active in your area go to www.christmasih.org/programs.

6. **Celebrate the Lunar New Year** observed throughout Asia by preparing Asian food and reading *Angel Child, Dragon Child*. If Asians are part of your congregation ask them to join in this celebration and tell how the Lunar New Year is celebrated in their country. If a local Asian group sponsors a public Lunar New Year festival, attend it as a class. (The Lunar New Year is usually in February or March.)

7. During Lent, many American congregations participate in the **One Great Hour of Sharing offering** of Church World Service. Fish-shaped coin banks and a collection of explanatory resources are provided for the children. As you work with these materials and the offering with third graders, focus on where some of the named service projects occur. Find them on a map. Collect your coins as a way of supporting neighbors all around the world.

8. **Create Welcome Kits for refugee children.** Invite each child to decorate and fill a shoe box or work as a class to decorate and fill a set number of boxes. Decide as a group what goes in each box (school supplies, caps for local sports teams, trinkets, tickets to a local children's attraction, postcards or flyers about things to do in your town, a wrapped cookie or candy snack, a welcome note from one child or the class, and so forth). Deliver the boxes to the office or invite someone to come get the boxes and tell you about their work in your community.

Go to: http://www.churchworldservice.org/refugees/ourprogram/local affiliateoffices to see if there is a church world service refugee resettlement program in your area. If there is no local connection there, call Catholic Social Services or a Lutheran church in your community as they tend to be involved in refugee resettlement.

9. **Exchange a visit with a group of children from another country or faith.** Consider children's classes from an ethnic congregation different from yours, a Jewish synagogue or temple, a Muslim community, or others. Have each group bring foods, games, music, other faith practices. Divide your time together so each group leads half of it. Your minister may know leaders in appropriate faith communities who could help you set this up.

Remember that the highest-impact projects are those the children choose or shape themselves. These projects empower them. They teach them that they can make a difference in the world. So, be responsive to their ideas about shaping these projects and alert to their ideas for other projects. The best project for the year may not be on this list!

Fill-In Activities for during the Year

1. Have on hand jigsaw puzzle-maps of the world, puzzles of different people and places, or the "I Never Forget a Face" matching game (see Resources). Early arrivers may enjoy working with and talking about these puzzles.

2. Order the twenty-four jumbo piece two-by-three-foot **"Our World Kid's Floor Puzzle"** from http://www.unicefusa.org/shop. Give each child in class one or two pieces, then challenge them to work together to assemble the puzzle. When the puzzle is complete, ask one child to remove his or her pieces. Ask the group if we still have the whole world. Discuss the temptation to ignore or leave out some people or groups or countries and the fact that the world is not complete without every one of us. Then have the puzzle available for early arrivers to assemble and discuss in weeks to come.

3. **Continue the "Praying Your Way around the World" activity** you started in the introductory session. On any week when you have a few extra minutes, name a country in the news and pray for the people in that country. As you talk about the people of that country, make a list of prayer concerns for them on the board or a big piece of paper. For the first few weeks, have an adult leader voice those concerns in prayer. As children see how it works, invite them to take turns voicing the prayers. One child may voice all the prayers for a week or a different child might voice each concern. Mark each country with a pushpin to keep track of all the places you have prayed about. Refer to the *Children's Mission Yearbook* (see Resources) to learn quickly about many countries.

4. **Keep a bulletin board of pictures** of people who are different or doing things in different ways in different places. Talk about the differences in individual pictures from week to week. These may be posted around the world map.

5. **Play games from around the world.** There are many books of such games available in school and public libraries. One to buy is *Kids around the World Play!*

6. If you are Presbyterian, but even if you are not, get a copy of the current **Children's Mission Yearbook**. Each annual version includes a cluster of activities related to a specific place where the Presbyterian Church is active for each week of the year. Activities include games, puzzles, crafts, recipes, and stories. Look up a country in the Table of Contents and select an activity to do after reading with the children about what the church is doing in that country.

7. **Read one of the story books listed in the Resource section about people conquering differences:** *Cooper's Lesson, The Hundred Dresses,* or *Smoky Night.*

8. **Say** *hello* **in as many languages as you can.** Ask class members to say hello in any languages they know.

9. **Near Christmas read *The Huron Carol* and if possible sing it together.**

Summary Session

Find and read 1 John 4:7 and 20. Starting with your "Let Us Love One Another" bulletin board, recall all you have explored and learned this year about God's worldwide family. (10 minutes)

Work together to create a worship service raising your concerns for all the different people around the world and dedicating your work to God. The service will need a praise psalm, a prayer of confession, a dedication of the projects, prayers for different people working together, and perhaps a song or two chosen by the group. Spend most of the class creating the various parts of the service. Then gather to celebrate the service together. (30 minutes)

There are several ways to prepare.
1. Set the materials and directions for each part of worship in a different part of the room. Divide into teams with an adult on each team. Give each team time to work a little on each part of worship. Clap your hands or ring a bell when it is time for teams to move to the next station. The first stop will need to be a little longer than the others for the group to get a solid start. All other stops, except the last one, can be briefer, allowing time for the children to read what has been done and add to it as they wish. At the last stop, teams need to not only edit what they find but also to prepare to lead it as the class worships together.
2. Assign each part of worship to one team to develop and lead. Each team will need adult leadership to get the task done well in the time available.

3. If your group is small, work together as a class to plan one part of worship after another. Before class, set the materials up around the class as in no. 1. During class, move from one to the next as you work.

Resources and directions for creating four parts of worship. (Provide marking pens or crayons rather than pencils for writing so that work can be read from a distance. Lined chart paper is a real help to young printers if it is available.)

Praise Psalm
    Create a praise psalm by completing these sentences:

    God, you created us all in your image.
    Thank you for making us all like you. We all . . .
    And thank you for all the ways we are so different.
    Some people . . .   Other people . . .
    God, you made each one of us and we praise you.

    During the worship service, the team that wrote the psalm or the last team to work on it stands before the class to read it together.

Prayer of Confession and Reminder of God's Forgiveness
    At the top of a piece of newsprint or poster board write, "God, we want to love one another, but sometimes we do not." At the bottom of the page, write, "We are sorry, God. Please forgive us and help us do better. Amen." Read the beginning and ending to this prayer. Then, with the children compose a series of sentences describing ways we mistreat people who are different from us. If several groups follow, they may add sentences.

    During the worship service, all read the whole prayer together from the poster. An adult or child then reminds the class, "God loves us and forgives always. Thank you, God." If passing the peace is a familiar practice in your congregation, pass the peace among the children.

Dedication
    At the top of a piece of newsprint, write "God, we . . . " At the very bottom of the page write "We give our work to you, O God." With the children complete that sentence with a list of activities and projects you did to connect different people this year.

    During the worship service the group that composed the list or the last group to work on it reads each item on the list as a separate sentence, e.g., "God, we ate many kinds of bread on World Communion Sunday." The whole class then responds to each sentence "We give our work to you, O God." The result is a litany of dedication.

Praise Psalm

God, you created us in your own image.
Thank you for making us like you.
We can...
_____

Thank you for the ways we are different, too.
Some people _____
Other people_____
Some people _____
Other people_____
Some people _____
Other people_____
Some people _____
Other people_____
God, you made each one of us and we praise you! Amen.

Dedication

God, we ...
_____
_____
_____
_____
_____
_____
_____
_____
_____
_____

God, we give our work to you.
We are sorry, God.
Please forgive us and help us do better. Amen

Prayer of Confession

God, we want to love one another, but sometimes we do not.
_____
_____
_____
_____
_____
_____
_____
_____
_____

We are sorry God. Please forgive us and help us do better. Amen.

Prayers for God's People

God, we pray for people who
_____
_____
_____
_____
_____
_____
_____
_____

Hear our prayers, O God.
We are sorry, God.
Please forgive us and help us do better. Amen

Prayers for God's People
>At the top of a big piece of newsprint, write, "God, we pray for people who . . ."
>At the very bottom of the page write, "Hear our prayers, O God." With the
>children complete the sentence at the top with prayers for different kinds of
>people and people who live in different places.
>
>During the worship service, the team that wrote these prayers or the last team
>to work on them will read the prayers one at a time with the whole class
>responding to each prayer by saying, "Hear our prayers, O God."

When all the parts of the service are prepared, arrange the posters in order where
all can use them as a bulletin. Arrange the room, sitting either in one large circle or
in pew-like rows. Use your bulletin board as a worship center and/or arrange several items recalling the year's work on a small table with a globe and a candle to
light. Review the order of the service with the children and add any fitting songs the
group wishes. Then settle into place, light the candle as a signal that worship is starting, and proceed. One sequence might be . . .

>Light the candle
>Praise psalm
>Song of praise—"He's Got the Whole World in His Hands"
>Read 1 John 4:7 and 1 John 4:20 (assign one child to do this in advance)
>Prayer of Confession and Promise of Forgiveness
>Passing the Peace
>Dedication of Our Work
>Prayers for God's People
>Teacher's Benediction: "Let us love one another for love is from God. Go in
>>Peace."

>(If you have not passed the peace earlier, the teacher may go from student to
>student shaking hands and saying, "[NAME], the peace of God be with you.")
> (10 minutes)

Resources

Angel Child, Dragon Child, Michele Maria Surat (New York: Scholastic, 1983).
>Ut, a lonely Vietnamese girl, is forced to work with the American boy who teases
>her to write about her life. The two connect and the boy initiates the idea of hold-
>ing a Vietnamese fair to raise the money needed to bring Ut's mother to this coun-
>try. The forty pages require two reading sessions at most.

Children Just Like Me, Barnabas and Anabel Kindersley (New York: Dorling
Kindersley, 1995).
>A picture and text book introducing the lives of specific children from all around
>the world. A good book to have in the room for early arrivers to enjoy.

Children's Mission Yearbook. (Order from Presbyterian Distribution Service at 1-800-524-2612 for $5.50 plus shipping.)

Each annual version includes a cluster of games, puzzles, crafts and recipes related to a specific place where the Presbyterian Church is active.

Cooper's Lesson, Sun Yung Shin (San Francisco: Children's Book Press, 2004).

A Korean-American boy wishes he were not "half and half." His frustrations come to a head in an encounter with a Korean store owner, who helps him value both parts of his identity. It can raise interesting discussions both about how mixed race children feel about themselves and how they are treated by other children.

The Hundred Dresses, Eleanor Estes (New York: Harcourt, Brace and World, 1944, reissued).

Wanda Petronski, who wears the same blue dress to school everyday, claims to have one hundred dresses in her closet. Popular Maddie and Peggy enjoy teasing her until her father writes a letter to the teacher telling her they are leaving town to live somewhere where they will not be teased. He also sends Wanda's drawings of one hundred beautiful dresses. Maddie and Peggy must deal with what they have done. The story is a bit dated and rather preachy in tone, but the relationships between the girls still ring true. Read this seven-chapter, seventy-three page book a chapter or two a week over several weeks.

The Huron Carol, Ian Wallace (Toronto: Ground Wood Hooks/ House of Anansi Press, 2006).

The biblical Christmas story is retold in the native Alaskan setting. This beautifully illustrated book parallels the Huron Christmas carol.

"I Never Forget A Face" Matching Game. Order from www.unicefusa.org/shop ($13 plus shipping).

A new twist on the old concentration game, featuring the faces of children from different cultures around the world, this is designed for children age three and up. Early arrivers who play it for a few minutes are gently reminded that God's family includes many different people all around the world.

Jonah and the Whale (and the Worm), Jean Marzollo (New York: Little, Brown, 2004).

Picture storybook of the biblical story with lots of essential background information in sidebars and humorous comments by octopi across the bottom of each page. The author added her ending to the story rather than leaving it open-ended as the Bible does.

Kids Around the World Play!: The Best Fun and Games from Many Lands, Arlette N. Braman (New York: Jossey-Bass, 2002).

A collection of games that children play around the world involving easily available equipment. Sidebars tell about the origins of the games and point out different ways each game is played in different countries.

"Our World Kid's Floor Puzzle." Order from www.unicefusa.org/shop ($15 plus shipping).
  A twenty-four jumbo piece, two-foot by three-foot jigsaw puzzle.

People, Peter Spier (New York: Bantam Doubleday Dell, 1980).
  Read the text on the first page and the last six pages of this book first to understand the author's point. Then, enjoy all the detailed pictures illustrating human differences in between. It is a book individuals or small groups enjoy savoring and discussing one page at a time. After the book is introduced in class, leafing through it is a good activity for early arrivers.

Portraits, Steve McCurry (London: Phaidon Press, 1999).
  A book of nearly 250 stunning portraits of people all around the world taken by a National Geographic photographer. Carefully separate the pages and store them in a zippable plastic bag for use on bulletin boards and in class activities.

Smoky Night, by Eve Bunting (Harcourt, 1999).
  Even the cats do not get along in this story where people stick with their own kind, until their building burns during the Los Angeles riots and they all pull together. Caldecott Award winner for artwork.

The Sneetches and Other Stories, Dr. Seuss (New York: Random House, 1961).
  The star-bellied and plain-bellied sneetches learn the hard way that they are really all the same.

CHAPTER SEVEN

Fourth Grade: Helping the Homeless

"People will build houses and get to live in them." (Isaiah 65:21 [GNT])

Introduction

HOMELESSNESS IS POVERTY TO THE EXTREME. People become homeless as a result of war, natural disasters, financial setbacks, even untreated mental illness or alcoholism. In the United States there is a deep stigma attached to being homeless. The unspoken assumption in this country is that anyone who tries can have the basics of life, including a home. Conversely, it is assumed that those who do not have the basics, including a home, have not tried very hard or are somehow "less" than the rest of us. These assumptions are clearly and subtly communicated to children in the media and through little acts like locking the car doors as we pass a beggar at the intersection. But the facts show that very few people choose or deserve to be homeless. Most are caught in things beyond their control: a factory has closed, medical bills have piled up, an illness or injury makes work impossible for the family breadwinner, and so on. For most people who get a little help, homelessness is a harrowing, and ultimately short-term experience.

One of the tasks of this year is to help the children cut through the stereotypes they absorb from our culture. They will need help reinterpreting what they see in the beggar on the street corner or the person camping outside over a steam grate. This will require good facts and thoughtful classroom conversations. It will be wise to have some of these conversations before contact with homeless persons so the children know what to expect and how to act and then to repeat conversations after their involvement to reflect on what they experienced and learned.

The second task is to introduce the children to some ways they can assist those who are currently homeless. The list of projects offers something for classes in all types of settings from urban to rural. You will have to determine which fit your situation or let them remind you of some service effort unique to your community in which the children could participate. A conversation with someone on the mission committee might be helpful here.

Finally, part of doing the work of loving our neighbors is organizing others to work with us. Fourth grade can be a good year for children to begin learning how to do this. Choose one project in which the children enlist the participation of others. They might conduct a congregation-wide collection of personal cleaning products to take to a shelter or oversee the preschoolers in collecting baby-care supplies during the Christmas season. Part of their work is to learn how to write and submit an article to the church newsletter, to make announcements in church school classes or minute for mission in worship, to think of other ways to promote their project, and finally to sort, pack, and deliver what they collected.

Possible goals for exploring this theme with fourth graders:
- to recognize those who are homeless in their community
- to name some causes of homelessness
- to identify some ways of assisting those who are homeless
- to identify some agencies in your community that work on behalf of those who are homeless
- to see themselves as people who can lead others in loving our neighbors

Introductory Session

Arrival activity: Invite children to help cut pictures of homes from magazines and newspapers. Go for as much variety as possible—igloos, tents, mobile homes, castles. *National Geographic* magazine is a good source. As you gather pictures, compare the different houses and what they offer the people who live there. (10 minutes)

And/or

Ask the children to draw pictures describing their own home. Talk about what they like most about their homes and hear any complaints about their homes, e.g., not enough space or enough bathrooms. Talk about what a home gives people. (10 minutes)

Read about God's dream of a home for all people. Read Isaiah 65:17-18 and 21-23 using the printed script. Ask students, "What does God intend for all people?" to explore exactly what is promised. Then ask students what is so good about this promise. (5 minutes)

GOD'S DREAM FOR ALL PEOPLE

The Lord says,

"I am making a new earth and new heavens.

The events of the past will be completely forgotten.

Be glad and rejoice forever in what I create . . ."

"The new Jerusalem I make will be full of joy, and her people will be happy.

I myself will be filled with joy because of Jerusalem and her people . . ."

"People will build houses and get to live in them—they will not be used by someone else.

They will plant vineyards and enjoy the wine—it will not be drunk by others.

Like trees, my people will live long lives.

They will fully enjoy the things that they have worked for.

The work they do will be successful, and their children will not meet with disaster.

I will bless them and their descendants for all time to come."

—Isaiah 65:17-19a and 21-23 from the *Good News Translation*

God's promise is not yet fulfilled. **Make a bulletin board describing many ways to be homeless**—war, natural disaster, poverty, illness. On strips of paper note the difficulties of being homeless.

1. Offer children a collection of pictures you have cut from magazines and newspapers depicting homeless people of all ages. (Search out pictures that indicate a variety of reasons the person is homeless—war, extreme poverty, lost job, natural disaster, mental illness, family abuse, migrant laborers.) Also offer strips of paper naming those reasons. Ask students to match pictures and reasons posting them on a bulletin board.

2. Do the **"Experiencing Homelessness"** exercise on page 89 or read one of the books describing the life of a homeless person.

3. As a class, write words that describe what it is like to be homeless on strips of colored paper and mount them around the border of the bulletin board.

4. Add a bubble titled "God's Dream" with Isaiah 65:21a printed on it.

(30 minutes)

Point out to children that we can join God in working toward that dream. **Introduce the chosen projects or offer several projects from which the class selects one or two** and begin making plans for the year's work together. (10 minutes)

As a closing, reread "God's Dream for All People" in unison and pray for the work you are about to undertake. (3 minutes)

Possible Projects

Before selecting projects for this year, find out which projects your group did as second and third graders. Many projects fit into several themes. If possible you want to expose the children to new experiences each year.

1. **Pack zippable plastic bags for people who approach cars begging.** In each bag put a few transit tokens, a coupon for a meal, and a card with information about where to get services for people in need in your community. Children could pack the bags to pass out from their own cars when they see people begging. Or, the class could make the bags and sell them to the congregation. (Charge enough for the bags to cover the transit tokens and meal coupon.) Selling the bags requires the class to get permission from the proper congregational committee. Publicize their effort in the newsletter and with posters, make the bags, and operate a booth from which to sell them.

2. **Host a party with games, crafts, and treats at a shelter for homeless families.** For example, on Valentine's Day take the supplies for making simple valentines, directions for a game, and some valentine cookies and punch for refreshments. The party need not last long to be a great success all around. Contact a local shelter to learn how and when this would be possible.

Experiencing Homelessness

Take the students on an imaginary journey into homelessness.

Announce to the class that they and their family just got kicked out of their house. They can take with them only what their family can squeeze into their car—and still have room for themselves.

Ask each child to make a list on a small piece of paper of what they will take with them.

Then announce that they will have to spend the night in the car. Ask one child with a larger family where each family member will sleep. Ask another child if he or she remembered to bring pajamas and a pillow. Ask a third, "What about a toothbrush?"

Ask the children to suggest places to park the car while they sleep in it. Hear suggestions and problems with them. Point out that the police will probably wake them up and tell them to move on from most places they park.

Ask students for words describing how they feel when they wake up in the car the next morning.

Now tell the children that they must go to school that morning. Ask, "Who brought school clothes and their book bag? Did you get your homework done?"

Announce that they will stop at McDonald's for breakfast. They will have to clean up and get ready for school in the McDonald's bathroom. Ask what their hair looks like and how they feel with no shower or bath.

Tell the children that as their parents pick them up after school, they tell them to go back and go to the bathroom. Dad has a meeting about a job and the rest of the family will have to wait in the car. There will be no bathrooms available.

Have the children describe what would happen as they and their brothers and sisters waited in the car for two hours during their dad's meeting.

Ask who is hungry, then announce that money is tight and the family will have to share sandwiches picked up at a gas station sandwich bar. No super-sized anything.

Now ask how it feels to face another night in the car.

After a week of this, what would the car look and smell like?

What if the situation lasted for months?

Ask each student to write a completion of the sentence "I learned that . . ." on the back of the paper on which they wrote their list. Share and discuss responses.

3. **Cook and serve a meal at a shelter or soup kitchen.** This is a good project for a school holiday, either the week after Christmas or one of the long weekends. Some shelters have a lead cook who needs volunteers to work with him or her. Other shelters will want you to cook and bring the food. They often provide menus and recipes. This sounds scarier than it is. Groups often enjoy cooking together at their church kitchen, then delivering and serving the food. Work with the shelter staff to plan ways for the children to talk with at least a few of the guests.

4. **Feed Habitat for Humanity volunteers.** Many communities have active chapters of Habitat for Humanity, which are building homes for those who cannot afford one on their own. Children can have limited presence at the work site for insurance reasons, but as a class you could make sandwiches and cookies with which to create lunches to deliver to the site. The group could eat at the site, possibly talk with both volunteers and the family for whom the house is being built, and see the house and the work in progress. The point is to see and contribute to a project that is very successful in helping people buy their own homes. For greater impact, time this to coincide with work planned by volunteers from your congregation.

5. **Collect items needed by people who are homeless.** The class will need to get permission from the proper committee; make collection boxes; publicize the collection with posters, announcements, and newsletter articles; tend the boxes; then pack and deliver what is collected. Possible collections include:

   - small shampoos, soaps, toothpaste, and other toiletries
   - new socks and underwear
   - mittens and gloves for all ages at Christmas
   - baby needs (disposable diapers, wipes, baby food, baby toys, etc.) Many preschool curricula suggest such collections in connection with the story of Jesus' birth in a stable. Fourth graders could organize and carry out this collection for the preschool department. (Warning: If this collection is done by the entire congregation, even a midsize congregation can gather more bulky diapers than a shelter can store. It is best to keep it a preschool department project.)

6. **Prepare health kits for people who are homeless because of natural disasters or war.** This is an especially good way for children to respond after a well-publicized disaster during the year. Go to the Church World Service website at www.churchworldservice.org. Click on the "Build a Village" icon, then "Give a Gift" icon, then "In Case of Emergency" to find clear directions for Health Kits and Clean Up after a Disaster Kits. Help each child compile a kit or work together to compile a set number and mail them. (Church World Service is the relief, development, and refugee assistance ministry of thirty-five Protestant, Orthodox, and Anglican denominations in the United States. Working in partnership with indigenous organizations in more than eighty countries, CWS works worldwide to meet human needs and foster self-reliance for all whose way is hard.)

Remember that the highest-impact projects are those the children choose or shape themselves. These projects empower them. They teach them that they can make a difference in the world. So, be responsive to their ideas about shaping these projects and alert to their ideas for other projects. The best project for the year may not be on this list!

Filler Activities for during the Year

1. **Invite a member of your congregation who has been on a house-building mission trip or has worked on a local Habitat project to tell your class about the experience.** Encourage your guest to tell about the person for whom the house was being built, what that volunteer actually did, and why he or she did it. This need not be a long conversation.

2. **Read and discuss one of the short story books listed in the Resource section** about different ways people are homeless. Many of these books look like young children's picture books. However, they are opportunities for in-depth discussions that raise the sensitivities of fourth graders. Keep several of them handy for use as needed.

3. **"What's in the Sack?"** (*Where the Sidewalk Ends* by Shel Silverstein) is a delightful, insightful poem with a great illustration of a man carrying a huge sack on his back. In the poem the man objects to the fact that all anyone ever asks about him is "What is in the sack?" He wishes for questions about him rather than the sack. Before reading the poem show the children several pictures of homeless people with lots of bags around them. Ask the children what they would like to ask those people. Then read the poem. Finally, as a class, brainstorm other questions to ask the people in the pictures. (The book is readily available in the children's section of most public libraries.)

4. **Read *The Biggest House in the World* and share the pictures.** Point out that the class has been paying attention to people who have too little house. Ask whether people, like the snail, can have too much house. There are no right or wrong answers here. It is simply an opportunity to challenge the children to stretch their thinking.

5. **Identify the baby Jesus as a homeless person.** Jesus was born in a stable in a town of overcrowded inns and immediately became a refugee in Egypt. The Advent Christmas season is an opportunity to help the children see through the Christmas tinsel to the unpleasantness of those situations and connect Jesus' situation with that of people who are homeless today. To do that try one of the following:

   • Visit a barn as a class. Decide where Mary and Joseph would have settled in this barn, then read the Christmas story there.

- Look at teaching pictures of the Nativity and read the related texts to explore Jesus' situation.

—Read Luke 2:1-7 (Jesus is born in a stable during a trip required to pay taxes). Look at a nativity picture to discuss what was nice and what was hard about having a baby in a barn.

—Display a picture of the flight into Egypt, read Matthew 2:13-14, and ask, "What was hard about this trip and about life in Egypt?" Connect Mary, Joseph, and Jesus' experience to those of refugees today.

6. **Learn about and even celebrate Las Posadas,** an annual Hispanic enactment of Mary and Joseph's search for a place to stay in Bethlehem. To learn about it, read *Las Posadas: An Hispanic Christmas Celebration*, especially pages 16–29. Point out the connection between this celebration of Mary and Joseph finding shelter with our welcoming homeless people seeking shelter today. Then turn your Christmas party into a Las Posadas party. Draw large figures of Mary and Joseph to tape on upside-down brooms to carry at the front of a processional. Or costume two children as Mary and Joseph (draw pieces of paper from a bowl to see who gets the parts). To incorporate singing in the processional, use the song on pages 24–25 of *Las Posadas* or the simpler song below. After acting out the search, have a party including a candy-filled piñata. This could be a class party. Or the fourth graders could host one or more younger children's classes explaining the celebration, leading the processional, and providing the party.

(To the tune of "I Saw Three Ships")

> Good innkeeper, may we come in,
> May we come in, May we come in,
> Good innkeeper, may we come in
> May we come in and find shelter?
>
> (*Response*)
> No, traveller, you can't come in
> You can't come in, you can't come in.
> No, traveller, you can't come in
> You can't come in and find shelter.
>
> (*Final response*)
> Yes, traveler, you can come in,
> You can come in, you can come in,
> Yes, traveler, you can come in,
> You can come in and find shelter.
> —adapted from a song by Marilyn Aberle

7. **Read and discuss** *December* for a picture of what Christmas might be like for a homeless mother and son today.

Summary Session: Happy Endings for People Who Are Homeless

From a collection of pictures of people who are homeless for a variety of reasons, ask each child to choose one picture. Have each child paste one picture in the center of a piece of a large sheet of stiff paper. Challenge the children to write a sentence describing the person's situation above the picture. Sitting in a circle, ask each child to show his or her picture and read the sentence. (5 minutes)

Invite the children to hear a biblical story about two homeless women. Promise that it has a happy ending. **Read the story of Ruth and Naomi** in "Two Brave Women" (*The Family Story Bible*). Read through the sentence, "Naomi worried that Ruth might work too hard and get sick." Then stop to ask:

- Why were Ruth and Naomi homeless?
- What problems did they face?
- What do you think they could do next?
- How do you think the story ends?

After discussing Ruth and Naomi's situation and guessing possible endings for the story, read the remainder of the story. After being sure they understand what happened,

- point out that it is a happy ending
- ask the children to identify what made the happy ending possible (Ruth and Naomi taking care of each other and Boaz's help)
- point out that happy endings are possible for other homeless people
- note together the happy endings you have heard about or been part of making happen during the year

(15 minutes)

If there is to be a children's report, plan together what you want to write about what you did. Select or draw any pictures you want to include. (10 minutes)

Together write a prayer dedicating what you did to God. On a chalkboard or big piece of paper, write two or three class-dictated and edited sentences telling God what you did and asking God to use your efforts to make a difference for the recipients. (10 minutes)

Ask the children to write a prayer below the picture of the homeless person on their poster. Encourage them to think about possible happy endings for their person. (5 minutes)

Close with a simple worship service raising class concerns about those who are homeless and dedicating what your class has done on behalf of homeless people this year. Use what you have created during this class session. Before you begin, gather reminders of what you have done this year on a small table. Add a Bible open to Isaiah 65 and a candle. Give each child a copy of the Isaiah 65 script from the introductory lesson (page 87) and seat them with their posters in a circle around the table. When all is ready:

Light a candle, saying, "God is with us always, wherever we go, wherever we live."

Read in unison the Isaiah 65 passage.

Ask each child to read a sentence describing the person in his or her poster picture. As a group, respond to each child, "Everybody needs a home."

One child or the whole group reads the class's posted prayer of dedication.

Ask each child to read aloud the prayer for the person in his or her picture. As a group, respond to each child, "Hear our prayers, O God."

The teacher/s move from child to child, taking each child's hands and saying to him or her, "Go in peace and love your neighbors."

Mount the children's posters on a bulletin board in your room or in a nearby hallway. Decide as a class what the title is and print it in place. (10 minutes)

Resources

A Shelter in Our Car, Monica Gunning (San Francisco: Children's Book Press, 2004).
 The strong urban art in this picture book draws fourth graders into this story of a young girl's life as she and her mother live in their car.

The Biggest House in the World, Leo Lionni (New York: Pantheon, 1968).
 In this classic picture book, a snail wishes himself into a house (shell) that becomes so big it finally keeps him from moving and thus causes his death. In a year when children are thinking about those who have no home, this book raises the thought-provoking question of how much home is enough.

Changing Places: A Kid's View of Shelter Living, Margie Chalofsky, Glen Finland, Judy Wallace (Mt. Ranier, Md.: Gryphon House, 1992).
 First-person comments of eight six- to twelve-year-olds about living in a shelter.

December, Eve Bunting (New York: Harcourt Brace, 1997).
 Experience Christmas Eve in the cardboard home of a homeless mother and son as they keep Christmas very simply and share it with a visitor, who they believe later was their Christmas angel who "changed their luck." The main value of the story is the account of the simple way this small family kept the true spirit of Christmas. A great choice for a December class session or class Advent celebration.

The Family Story Bible, Ralph Milton (Louisville: Westminster John Knox Press, 1997).

This storybook is the source of the story about Ruth and Naomi used in the Summary Session.

Fly Away Home, Eve Bunting (New York: Clarion Books, 1991).

Though this book is aimed at slightly younger readers, it offers a clear presentation from a boy's perspective of what it would be like to live in an airport while homeless. It could be an especially good discussion starter with children who frequent large metropolitan airports.

Gleam and Glow, Eve Bunting (San Diego: Harcourt, 2001).

This story of a family homeless because of war is aimed at younger children, but is a clear account about what happens (with sensitive pictures). It could be a good discussion starter with fourth graders.

Homeless in America, Michael A.W. Evans (Washington D.C.: Acropolis Books, 1988).

A book of large black and white photos describing the life of the homeless in America. The book is out of print, but I found it in the adult section of my local public library. On the day I checked, seven new or used copies of the book were available from subcontractors on Amazon.com. The pictures provide a glimpse of life in shelters and on the street for both adults and children. Leave it available in the room for early arrivers to flip through. Look at some of the pictures as a class before visiting a shelter.

Las Posadas: An Hispanic Christmas Celebration, Diane Hoyt-Goldsmith (New York: Holiday House, 1999).

This book begins by describing the religious life of a family in a New Mexican village, then focuses on the meaning and celebration of Las Posadas. Recipes and music for a Las Posadas song are included. The book is illustrated with lively, colorful photographs of children participating in the festival.

The Night of Las Posadas, Tomie DePaola (New York: Putnam, 1999).

This story's focus on a miraculous Mary and Joseph leading a town's Las Posadas procession when the scheduled couple is stuck in a snowstorm is a bit of a stretch. But it could be good to read at a Las Posadas party with children who already know about this celebration.

Someplace to Go, Maria Testa (Morton Grove, Ill.: Albert Whitman and Company, 1996).

An account of one afternoon in the life of a homeless older elementary boy named Davey. After school he is on his own until the soup kitchen opens for supper, his mother gets off work, and his older brother catches up with him after his job hunt. The straightforward language and believable art offers children a sensitive look into the realities homeless children their age face every day.

Things to Make and Do for Advent and Christmas, (Louisville: Bridge Resources, 1997).

See page 92 for a song taken from this resource to sing at a Las Posadas party for younger children.

Uncle Willie and the Soup Kitchen, DyAnne Disalvo-Ryan (New York: Morrow, 1991).

On a day off from school a boy accompanies his uncle through preparing and serving lunch at a soup kitchen. Though the book is designed for slightly younger children, it is a great discussion starter with fourth graders and good preparation for work at a soup kitchen.

www.trevorscampaign.org is the web page of a Philadelphia effort to meet the needs of the homeless that grew out of the concerns of Trevor, an eleven-year-old boy, who in response to news about homeless people freezing on the streets, first took his blanket and pillow to a homeless person and then organized collections of food and blankets. His efforts were the beginning of something that is now much bigger than one boy, but which continues to honor him by using his name. This is an adult website. Rather than go there with children, educate yourself there, then tell the story to the children.

CHAPTER EIGHT

Fifth Grade: It Is Not Fair! Standing Up for Justice

"Let justice roll down like waters . . ." *(Amos 5:24)*

Introduction

"IT IS NOT FAIR!" IS A COMMON CRY among elementary school children. Most often it is a demand for justice for themselves. They want to get their fair share of the fries, to have the same privileges their friends have, and to do what they want to do as often as possible. But by the fifth grade, children are ready to build on their own desire for fair treatment to wish and work for fair treatment for others. Fifth graders encounter unfair treatment among peers at school and unfair situations in the larger world. They can move from acknowledging that all people are God's loved and valued children, to recognizing that not all people are treated that way. With help, they can look around themselves to identify those who are not treated fairly and begin to find simple ways to help make needed changes.

Fifth graders can also begin to understand the difference between deeds of compassion (taking care of those caught in unfair situations) and ministries of justice (working to change the situation that causes the injustice). They are familiar with the first and can begin to claim the second. Every time they identify an unfair situation and challenge it with at least a little success, they begin to see themselves as people who can make a difference and are empowered to try again.

HEADS UP! This book offers no activities or projects related to justice for people with a homosexual orientation. It is a topic most fifth-grade church school teachers would avoid bringing up. But, it is a subject the fifth graders might bring up. Name-calling and vicious teasing based on vulgar sexual language is common among preteens. (Often they do not understand the meaning of the slurs they hurl at each other.) If the subject comes up, listen carefully to what is said and steer the conversation accordingly. The main concern is likely to be unjust name-calling. In that case, collect other unjust names based on racial, ethnic, and economic situations and then discuss the larger issues of prejudice and bullying.

Possible goals for exploring this theme with fifth graders:

- to identify some injustices in the world and describe how they affect individuals
- to explain the difference between compassion ministries and justice ministries
- to claim God's call for people to work to end injustice
- to experience working to alleviate at least one injustice

Introductory Session

Begin class with an **UNFAIR experience**. Ask if they are happy where they are sitting. Then, declare that no one may change seats. Give one table or one child a big bowl of donut holes or similar treat, other tables or individuals one treat per person, and one table or individual no treat at all. Then read aloud Amos 5:24. "Let justice roll down like waters, and righteousness like an ever-flowing stream." Give the table or person that got the big treat the included word search based on the text (on page 99). Give the one-treat person/s or group/s a set of cards to arrange in the proper sequence (one word from the text written on each card). Finally give the table or child who got no treat a Bible from which to copy the text. There should be serious cries of "Unfair!" by now. Ask the class what is unfair and why it is unfair. Give the slighted tables extra of the food treat, then proceed to the next activity. (10 minutes)

Before class arrange **"It's Not Fair!" pictures** along a wall. Include magazine and newspaper pictures of hungry and poor children, homeless people sleeping out-of-doors, people who have been injured in wars or violence, pictures that indicate racial injustices, and so forth. Try to have at least a dozen pictures raising a variety of issues. Title this display, "It Is Not Fair!" Give each child a half sheet of paper and pencil. Send them to the wall to find one picture they think is particularly unfair or something that picture reminds them of that is unfair. Then ask them to write a sentence about it. For example: children are dying for lack of food. (5 minutes)

Together create an **"It's Not Fair" psalm** by each child by reading statements and by the whole group responding to each statement with "It is not fair, God!" (5 minutes)

Together look up, read aloud and answer questions about **Micah 6:6-8** ("With what shall I come before the LORD . . . what does the LORD require of you but to do justice, and to love kindness, and to walk humbly with your God?")

- Working from your experiences in this session and consulting a dictionary, define justice.

What God Wants

```
L  W  R  Y  T  I  K  Y  M  H  G  Q  T  S
J  D  A  Q  P  O  Z  Q  Y  N  R  C  U  S
V  I  S  T  J  V  J  L  I  J  C  S  B  E
R  T  K  N  E  Q  N  W  O  D  G  D  Y  N
H  M  Z  G  D  R  O  X  T  Y  T  W  I  S
L  J  X  A  Z  L  S  E  Y  H  W  Q  W  U
W  E  K  D  F  W  L  X  R  R  V  J  J  O
P  R  W  R  T  K  R  S  M  M  T  M  Z  E
Z  R  E  S  P  M  L  R  E  K  B  R  X  T
G  V  L  T  Q  S  O  U  F  K  R  Z  H  H
E  E  X  R  P  L  J  U  S  T  I  C  E  G
A  F  Q  E  L  T  D  A  N  D  X  L  E  I
A  L  S  A  N  Q  R  V  F  J  E  L  J  R
G  X  X  M  W  T  N  G  T  E  F  Q  O  H
```

AN	EVERFLOWING	RIGHTEOUSNESS
AND	JUSTICE	ROLL
BUT	LET	STREAM
DOWN	LIKE	WATERS

"But let justice roll down like waters,
and righteousness like an ever-flowing stream"
Amos 5:24

What Does the Lord Require?

- What is the difference in kindness and justice?
  (Kindness treats people caught in unjust situations gently while justice seeks to change the unjust system that causes the pain. Both are important work. This year the focus is on justice.)
- Does God care about things that are unfair?
- What does God expect us to do when we see things that are unfair?

Conclude the Bible study by reading Jesus' announcement of his ministry in **Luke 4:16-21** ("He has anointed me to bring good news to the poor . . . release to the captives . . . sight to the blind . . . and to let the oppressed go free . . .") and asking the students to put it into their own words. (15 minutes)

Introduce potential justice projects for the year and begin plans. Choose from the projects described here. Or, invite the chair of your congregation's justice committee to describe your congregation's projects and suggest ways the fifth graders could get involved in them. Then as a class select projects from those. (10 minutes)

Learn the song, "What Does the Lord Require" (page 100). Begin by helping students put the three instructions of the song into their own words and answer these questions.

- How do we do justice today?
- How do we love kindness?
- What does it mean to walk humbly with God?

(5 minutes)

Maintain and add to the wall of pictures during the year. Add Bible verses you encounter in other studies, new pictures from the news, and so on. Begin by posting copies of the two Bible passages read today among the pictures.

Possible Projects

1. Call your congregation's ministry committee chair to find out what **justice efforts your congregation is supporting or involved in.** Ask for ideas on how the fifth-grade class can get involved. Invite the committee chair to talk with the class during the introductory session about the congregation's justice work and to outline the projects in which they might get involved. The class can then select project/s based on this information. Or invite individuals involved in specific projects to speak about their particular effort.

2. **Buy Fair Trade products.** Learn about organizations that sell products guaranteed to be made by people who got paid fairly for their work and support them with your purchases.

   - Ten Thousand Villages sells crafts and toys from small craft cooperatives around the world. Learn about its history and products at www.tenthousandvillages.com. Use the Store Locator to find stores near you. If there is a store near you (160 stores in 36 states), plan a holiday class shopping trip before Christmas. Encourage fifth graders to come prepared to do some or all of their Christmas shopping. If there is no store or festival (one-time sale) nearby, get the catalog and do your shopping by mail. After your shopping trip or when the order comes in, pray over all the people involved in making and marketing these gifts and the people who will receive them.

- Buy your church at least one Fair Trade soccer ball or football. Unlike many balls, Fair Trade balls are stitched by adults rather than exploited children. On amazon.com click on Sports & Outdoors, then search for "fair trade balls."

- Sell Divine Chocolate in your congregation for a "Just and Loving" Valentine's Day. Learn about this Ghanaian fair trade company and its products at www.divinechocolate.com. Fifth graders may wrap each bar with a red ribbon or decorate each bar with red heart stickers for the sale. (Divine Chocolate is also available through Ten Thousand Villages.)

- The cutting edge of fair trade shopping as I write is fair trade clothing. Go to the Internet with your class to search for "fair trade clothes." Some companies, such as Fair Indigo, tell you where each item is made and something about the factory in which it is made. Find a small item, maybe a hat or T-shirt, each student could buy and wear. Or simply surf the fair trade clothes websites as a consciousness-raising activity. A fun way to begin either of these activities is to check the labels in clothing the children are wearing to see where each item was made.

3. **Contribute to a Justice Project.** Alternative Gifts International (on the web: www.alternativegifts.org) creates a catalog of gift coupons with which people can make donations to philanthropic projects "in honor of" friends on birthdays, Christmas, and so on. Select from this year's offerings one that is justice related and raise money for it as a class. This need not be done as a gift at holiday time, but simply as a donation to an important effort.

   - Consider setting aside all the money the fifth graders would have spent on sodas during the six weeks of Lent to fund this justice donation. Children may give up the sodas in order to put the money into this project or they may keep a record of how many sodas they drink and contribute based on that number.

4. **Make space for people with challenging physical needs.** As a class, do an accessibility audit of your congregation's building. Borrow a wheelchair and see where it is hard to go in it. Do the same with crutches and blindfolds. Interview members of the congregation for whom such challenges are part of life to find out what is most challenging about participating fully in your congregation's activities. If you find one or two items that you believe your

class could provide and/or campaign for, work on getting them as a class. Possibilities to consider include: grab bars for bathrooms, ramps into the building or in hallways, hearing assistive devices, large-print worship bulletins or large-print hymnals, and so forth. Another special need to consider is a baby-changing table in a convenient bathroom.

5. **Name-calling and bullying** are common injustices among middle school children. No Name-Calling Week is one attempt to help students combat it. Though designed to be used in public schools, some of the resources could be used as a session at church. Go to www.nonamecallingweek.org, then click on Resources. Lesson 7, "Don't Just Stand By," offers guidelines for standing up for another child who is being bullied and situations in which to practice those guidelines.

Remember that the highest-impact projects are those the children choose or shape themselves. These projects empower them. They teach them that they can make a difference in the world. So, be responsive to their ideas about shaping these projects and alert to their ideas for other projects. The best project for the year may not be on this list!

Filler Activities for during the Year

1. **Invite a member of the congregation who has worked on a justice campaign to tell the children about it.**

2. **Strategize ways of responding to injustices at school.** Write each of the situations below on an index card and put it in a box or bag. On Sundays when you have a few extra minutes, have one student draw a card for the class to discuss. Add cards describing injustices of which you are aware or which come up during the year.
   - A group of boys are playing Keep Away with a hat snatched from the head of a younger boy. What can you do?
   - A girl at your school wants to play on the school wrestling team. She is really good. Some kids think she should be able to wrestle if she wants. Others are laughing at her and making jokes about her. What do you think? What will you say and do? NOTE: Women's wrestling is an Olympic sport and girls' wrestling is a growing sport in schools. Some school systems now have girls' leagues. In others, girls are earning places on boys' teams.
   - Two girls start a "clothes club" in which they make fun of the clothes other girls wear. You know girls they are ridiculing are really hurt. What can you do?
   - There is a kid that everyone in your class makes the butt of every joke and teases. The kid does nothing to deserve this treatment. It just sort of got started and keeps going. What can you do to stop this unfair treatment?
   - In your school everyone gets Christmas and Easter as holidays. But Jewish kids get an unexcused absence if they stay out to celebrate Passover or

Yom Kippur. Muslim kids also get unexcused absences if they stay out to celebrate Eid. Is that fair? Why or why not?

- Which racial groups are found among students and teachers in your class at school? How are people of the various races treated? What keeps people of different races apart? What are things they can easily do together? Is there anything you could do to help people of different races get along better?
- Prejudice is deciding what a person is like before you get to know him or her. Which of the following prejudice triggers causes most trouble in your class—too fat or thin? skin color? clothes? grades? too quiet or too talkative? Why does that trigger such prejudice?

3. **Read, discuss, and write poetry about standing up for justice.** Begin by reading this version of Rev. Martin Niemoller's famous poem. Niemoller wrote this during the rise of Hitler in Germany when people had to decide whether to follow Hitler's plan of destroying all nonwhite Germans. This poem has been rephrased since then to call people to stand up for the rights of others in their own time. Next read *Terrible Things*, by Eve Bunting, a picture-book rephrasing of the poem using animals in the forest. Then challenge the class to come up with their own versions of the verses for fifth graders in their town and school.

> *First they came for the communists, and I did not speak out—*
> *because I was not a communist;*
> *Then they came for the socialists, and I did not speak out—*
> *because I was not a socialist;*
> *Then they came for the trade unionists, and I did not speak out—*
> *because I was not a trade unionist;*
> *Then they came for the Jews, and I did not speak out—*
> *because I was not a Jew;*
> *Then they came for me—*
> *and there was no one left to speak out for me.*
> —attributed to Rev. Martin Niemoller, 1945

4. **Read aloud in class a biography of a person who worked for justice** if needed over several weeks' time. See the Resources list.

5. **Give yourselves a prejudice check-up.** FAIR is a website curriculum that includes stories that can be told by a teacher or read on a free Powerpoint presentation. Each story includes a variety of people interacting with each other. Students are asked to describe the person they visualize for each person in the story and then are challenged to evaluate their assumptions about gender, age, and race. Read or present one story and discuss it in ten to fifteen minutes. Find the stories at www.fair.cahs.colostate.edu, clicking on Curriculum Overview, then the first tent "Images in Our Mind." If the class works well with the stories, check out the other tents for additional activities.

6. **At Thanksgiving read and discuss** *Crossing Bok Chitto* in which Choctaws help a slave family escape when they learn that the mother is to be sold. Both the Choctaws and the slaves must act with great courage to claim justice.

7. **During Advent read and discuss** *The Christmas Menorahs*. The book describes the response of the children and adults of Billings, Montana when a hate group threw a rock through the menorah-decorated window of a Jewish ten-year-old. You may find this book in your public library.

8. **During Lent/Easter as you study the Holy Week stories, identify ways Jesus was the victim of injustices.** For example, witnesses at his trial could not agree on their testimony, but the Sanhedrin (religious court) found Jesus guilty anyway (Mark 14:55-56). Pilate believed Jesus did not deserve the death sentence, but allowed it rather than risk trouble with the religious leaders who wanted Jesus dead (Mark 15:1-15). Religious leaders sent people into the crowd to be sure they called for Barabbas rather than Jesus to be freed (Mark 15:6-15). Even one of the thieves killed with Jesus insisted that Jesus did not deserve to be crucified (Luke 23:39-43).

9. If a justice issue that really gets the attention and concern of your students comes up in your community or world during the year, **discuss it and be ready to write a letter** to an appropriate person or take other action as a class. Acting on something as it arises can empower students more than any planned activity or project.

10. **Sing** "What Does the Lord Require?" (page 100).

11. **Use the topical index in your congregation's hymnal/worship songbook to find songs about justice.** Read through at least a few of them, asking the children what each one is saying about justice. If possible, invite a musician to help you sing a few. As a group choose one or two favorites and send them to the pastor and choir director, asking if they could be sung in worship sometime.

Summary Session

If there is to be a children's report or pamphlet, plan together an article about what you did for justice this year. Select or draw any pictures you want to include. (15 minutes)

Create a bulletin board display of justice posters. Before class cover a bulletin board with light-colored paper with a large blue waterfall down the center. Also prepare a blue poster with the words of Amos 5:24 printed on it. With students brainstorm a list of "justice needed here" situations or places. Refer to your "It's Not Fair" display and justice projects for ideas. Record your list on a chalkboard. Then ask each student to select one item from the list for which to make a poster calling for justice. Posters may be just words or may include symbols and illustrations. Mount the posters around the central waterfall on the bulletin board. (20 minutes)

OR

Create a worship service with which to dedicate what you have done and learned.
(45 minutes)

To prepare:

Place reminders of what you have done for justice during the year on a small table. Add a Bible opened to Amos 5:24 or other verse of the class's choice and a candle.

On a chalkboard, compose a prayer of dedication thanking God for what you have learned, asking God's blessing on what you did for justice, and asking God to help each of you stand up for justice in the future.

As a class decide which of the following scripture texts to read.
> Micah 6:6-8
> Luke 4:16-21
> Matthew 15:12-14

Turn the bulletin board into a litany with each student reading the phrase on his or her poster and the class responding with "Let justice roll down like waters, and righteousness like an ever-flowing stream."

If you did the Filler Activity identifying justice songs, select one or two to sing during your service today. If you learned "What Does the Lord Require?" consider it.

Follow an order of worship something like this:

Light the candle

Sing a justice song (if you have learned one)

"Let justice roll down like waters" litany (based on bulletin board)

Read the selected scriptures

Sing another justice song

Pray your prayer of dedication, reading from the board.

Charge and Benediction led by a student or teacher reading "One" and rest of the class reading "*All*."

> One: Go now to do justice.
> *All*: *We will.*
> One: Go now to act with kindness toward all people.

All: *We will.*
One: Go now to walk humbly with God.
All: *We will.*
One: And remember that God will be with you always.
All: *We will.*
One: Amen.

Resources

The Christmas Menorahs, Janice Cohn, D.S.W. (Morton Grove, Ill.: Albert Whitman and Company, 1995; paperback, 2000).
An account of a true event in Billings, Montana in which citizens of all faiths displayed menorahs in their windows after a group of skinheads threw a rock through the bedroom window of a young Jewish boy in town. The book clearly discusses ways to respond to people who hate.

Crossing Bok Chitto, Tim Tingle (El Paso: Cinco Puntos Press, 2006).
Friendship between a young Choctaw girl on one side of the river Bok Chitto and a young slave on the other open the way for the slave family to escape across the river when the mother is to be sold away. Beautiful illustrations show how the Choctaws helped that happen.

God Said Amen, Sandy Eisenberg Sasso (Woodstock, Vt.: Jewish Lights Publications, 2000).
A prince whose country has plenty of water and no oil and a princess whose country has plenty of oil but needs water each refuse to make the first move toward sharing their resources. A better life for all is lost as long as the vanity of these two proud leaders stands in the way. For mature fifth graders, this is an opportunity to discuss how our personal failures can get in the way of justice for all.

The Hundred Dresses, Eleanor Estes (New York, Harcourt, Brace and World, 1944, reissued).
Wanda Petronski, who wears the same blue dress to school every day, claims to have one hundred dresses in her closet. Popular Maddie and Peggy enjoy teasing her until her father writes a letter to the teacher telling her they are leaving town to live somewhere where they will not be teased. He also sends Wanda's drawings of one hundred beautiful dresses. Maddie and Peggy must deal with what they have done. The story is a bit dated and rather preachy in tone, but the relationships between the girls still ring true. Read this seven-chapter, seventy-three-page book a chapter or two a week over several weeks.

A Picture Book of Harriet Tubman, David A. Adler (New York: Holiday House, 1991).
A picture biography of Harriet Tubman, the great Underground Railroad guide known as Moses to the slaves she led to freedom. This is another good book to

read in turns in class. The book about Sojourner Truth with all its language about what is fair would be the first choice.

A Picture Book of Sojourner Truth, David A. Adler (New York: Holiday House, 1994).
A picture biography of Sojourner Truth, who began life as a slave and protested a variety of injustices during her long life. She is repeatedly reported to say, "It is not fair!" Before reading this, instruct students to listen for "unfair situations" that Sojourner recognized and what she did about them. In the discussion, note how many issues she spoke to or acted on remained problems for years later. Reading this book and discussing it could be a good activity for a substitute teacher teaching on short notice.

So Far from the Sea, Eve Bunting (New York: Clarion Books, 1998).
A picture book describing a family remembering the death of the grandfather during the Japanese internment of World War II. Though it is aimed at slightly younger readers, the discussions in the book about how unfair it was both for their patriotic grandfather to be interned and for the Japanese to attack Pearl Harbor can be used to encourage discussion among fifth graders about how unfairness spawns more unfairness on all sides.

The Story of Ruby Bridges, Robert Coles (New York: Scholastic, 1994, 2004).
Many fifth graders will have encountered this story of a young African American girl who was involved in the earliest days of school integration. Hearing it again as part of a focus on justice gives them a chance to reclaim the possibility that children can make big contributions and to explore the need for justice seekers to also be forgivers.

Terrible Things: An Allegory of the Holocaust, Eve Bunting (Philadelphia: Jewish Publication Society, 1989).
This story is based on Martin Niemoller's poem about people failing to stand up for others when they are victimized, only to find there is no one left to stand up for them when they are victimized. In this picture book, the animals in a forest, rather than people, cower when "the terrible things" come for different kinds of animals.

www.tolerance.org is a gold mine of resources and lesson plans related to tolerance of diversity for children kindergarten through grade twelve. Click on For Teachers, Classroom Activities for a collection of almost 250 lesson plans on everything from racism to bullying to sensitivity to economic differences. This is designed for public school teachers, but many of the resources can be used in churches.

PART FOUR

A Word about the Partnership between Families and Congregations

In its study on how people grow into mature faith, the Search Institute identified four key experiences for children and youth.

1. frequent conversations with mom about her faith
2. frequent conversations with dad about his faith
3. frequent family worship both at home and in the sanctuary
4. frequent family serving projects

Serving others shapes us. Serving others with our families shapes us more profoundly than serving with our peers. So congregations serve children and their parents well when we draw them into service as families and when we equip them to make loving neighbors part of daily life at home.

Congregations can invite families with children into serving ministries together. Rather than always sending children on the Hunger Walk with their church school classes, sometimes encourage families to raise money and walk as families. Schedule monthly or quarterly Saturday afternoon serving projects designed for families with children. Suggest that all members of the family rather than just one adult sign the family's pledge card. Plan family mission trips as well as youth and adult mission trips. Keeping families together in serving ministries gives them a much-valued chance to work together, creates opportunities for faith-sharing conversations between parents and children, offers parents ways to model neighborly love for their children, gives children the security they need to try new activities in new places, and tends to be fun.

Congregations also serve children when they equip parents to make loving neighbors part of daily life at home. Each of the seven disciplines in this book (refer to Part One) needs to be pursued at home as well as at church, and most parents appreciate some help doing this. Printing the blurbs provided in this book in a place where parents as well as teachers will read them is one way to help. Preschool teacher training that focuses on how to help children build relationship skills also serves as parent training. (In fact, such a merger of teacher and parent training can attract parents to teaching.) An occasional workshop encouraging parents in the practice of the other disciplines for raising children to love their neighbors can be offered on its own or fit into adult church school classes.

Children benefit when families and congregations are intertwined and what is taught and promoted at church reflects what is taught and modeled at home.

Chapter Nine

A Workshop for Parents Who Are
Raising Children to Love Their Neighbors

Catching the Vision

Before class give each of the opening readings to one parent to read when called upon.

To open the subject of the class remind parents of its title. Then ask them to listen to the following short readings in search for their own answers to the question, "What do you want for your children in the area of compassion?

> "I will pour out my spirit on all flesh;
> your sons and your daughters shall prophesy,
> your old men shall dream dreams,
> and your young men shall see visions,
> Even on the male and female slaves,
> in those day, I will pour out my spirit." (Joel 2:28)

"The LORD has told us what is good. What he requires of us is this: to do what is just, to show constant love, and to live in humble fellowship with our God." (Mic. 6:8 [GNT])

"A teacher of the Law . . . asked, which is the greatest commandment in the Law?" Jesus answered, 'Love the Lord your God with all your heart, with all your soul, and with all your mind.' This is the greatest and the most important commandment. The second most important commandment is like it: 'Love your neighbor as you love yourself.' The whole Law of Moses and the teachings of the prophets depend on these two commandments." (Matt. 22:35-40 [GNT])

Also read the promises parents make at a baptism in your congregation, if they pertain to raising compassionate children.

As a group list on newsprint or a chalkboard answers for the question, "What do we want for our children in the area of compassion?"

Three Ways to Implement the Vision

1. Helping Children Learn How to Be Loving Neighbors

Using the material on pages 3 to 6 present a mini-lecture describing teaching children relationship skills in order to equip them for ministries of compassion. Explore the significance of teaching these skills not as manners that help a child succeed, but as ways we love our neighbors. Connect these skills with issues such as tolerance and justice.

Make a list on the board of ways we teach children relationship skills. Start with the items in the list below, taking time to talk about how we work with our children on each one. Welcome parent additions to the list. When the list feels complete, work through it a second time, discussing how each item is related to encouraging compassion in children and identifying strategies for each one that direct the child toward compassion.

Taking turns
Sharing
Helping out
Being a friend
Meeting new people
Treating kindly the people we meet every day
"It's not fair!" claims
(Not) grabbing
Giving gifts and love to others

Give parents a copy of "A Beginner's Vocabulary for Caring" (page 18). Ask them to give phrases in which we can use those words at home. Encourage them to use the words frequently, perhaps posting them on the refrigerator door as a reminder.

2. Becoming a "Pitch In Family"

Point out that a key way we help children become helpers is by expecting help at home. Introduce the term "Pitch In Family" as a family that expects all members to pitch in appropriately to get the needed work done.

Together make a list of household tasks children can be expected to perform and discuss the ages at which children can be expected to perform them. There are few right and wrong answers here. The conversation between parents will probably prove thought provoking for all. When the list is complete, point out that it is important both to interpret household chores as "helping" to children and to affirm the children in their work. As a group, share specific phrases and strategies that can be used in doing this.

3. Taking Care of Other People as a Family

Present material from the introduction of this section about the importance of children getting involved in serving others with their parents. Then help parents explore specific ways their families can do such serving together. Try some or all of the following:

- list activities of your congregation in which families can serve together
- ask parents to describe service projects their families have tried successfully
- brainstorm ideas including the above and "things people have heard about"

Conclusion

There is nothing new and startlingly different in any of this. The challenge for parents is to recognize that all the work we are doing with our children is really more about compassion than about manners. With this vision, we follow all these disciplines with a new spirit. When we do, there is inspiration for the days when it is harder and guidance when we are not sure what we are doing or why.

Final Word

Exciting neighborly activities such as mission trips and philanthropic projects in which teens are asked to manage thousands of dollars to benefit other people are the cutting edge of youth ministry. Too often teenagers respond to these experiences with, "I never knew this was out there!" Instead of finding these experiences a logical extension of what they have been doing throughout their childhood at church, they see in them something new and different.

Searching for a mission scope and sequence for children has taught me that we need to be much more intentional about drawing our children and their families into caring for their neighbors from their earliest days. Just as we plan careful ways to draw children into worship and to teach them the stories of the faith, we must plan ways to draw them into loving their neighbors. We cannot simply expect that they, or at least some of them, will one day choose serving others as their way of expressing their faith. Instead, we must pay careful attention to how children at each age can care for others. We must identify the skills they need and teach them those skills. We must identify the concerns of each age that relate to loving others and help children make the connections at that age. And we must invite them to oversee, overhear, and personally participate in the life and ministry of their loving congregation. Doing all this is the way we raise them to follow Jesus' second great commandment, "Love your neighbor as you love yourself."

I share this at this point not as a fully developed theory to be debated, but as a starting point for lots of ongoing conversations and work. The seven disciplines, teacher workshops for preschool teachers, projects for preschoolers, and elementary enrichment curricula are all works in process in a variety of congregations and in a number of caring adult hearts and minds. The invitation to you is to join the process. The final word is not "therefore," it is "and . . ."